Financial Fund of Knowledge

by
Michael Reiman,
CFS, RFC, DIA

and
Max Adams,
ESQ., LUTCF, CRFA

Financial Fund of Knowledge

For information:

Reiman Publishing

13410 Preston Road, Ste A-103

Dallas, TX 75240

0-9792794-0-2

Previously printed through Heliographica under ISBN# 1-933037-655

Printed in the United States of America

This book is dedicated to our valued clients and to our loved ones.

Financial Fund of Knowledge

Disclaimer

This book is written to provide general thoughts and advice on some of the financial and professional challenges you face. It is not meant as a substitute for advice from qualified professionals who are familiar with your individual needs and situation. You should not take any of the steps contemplated in this book, or act on any of the advice presented in this book, without consulting a financial advisor, a tax professional, and an attorney, all of which may involve one or more persons or firms. In addition, federal and state laws governing some of the activities described in this book will change after the printing of this book, so be sure you have sought up-to-date advice before proceeding with any of the transactions described in this book.

A Word about Pronoun Reference

We have chosen to alternate the use of pronouns between masculine and feminine to avoid the cumbersome use of "she/he". Please note that the use of one gender should be considered to refer to both genders throughout the book.

Acknowledgments

Writing a book is a huge undertaking. We could never have completed such a monumental task without the help of numerous people.

We wish to convey our deepest thanks to the following individuals who helped us take this book from idea to reality: Emily Jenkins, for help and expertise in guiding us through this process. You are so knowledgeable, and we value your insight. Dr. Kiki Reiman, you have been an invaluable resource. Your advice and recommendations made this book better suited to our clients. We truly appreciate your time and efforts on our behalf. Howard Hacker, for your advice and your beneficial input that helped shape the manuscript. Your expertise increased the value of the information in the book. Michael Dubner, we are so gracious for all of your guidance regarding publishing and copyright issues. You really went above and beyond.

We would also like to thank our many clients for providing us with the concept for writing this book. Although our clients often come to us for insight, it is our clients who have given us the insights into the physician's life that helped us refine our practices and led to the publication of this book. We appreciate your continued support and look forward to continuing our relationships with you.

We'd also like to express our thanks to our friends and family who supported us in many ways while we wrote this book. Your continued support allows us to provide the best to our writing and our clients. Thanks for supporting us through this process. We especially want to thank our wives, Melissa and Lisa, for encouraging us to take on this project.

Table of Contents

Introduction...xv

Chapter One: The Personal Money Management Strategy.......... 1

Stay Organized.. 2

Protect Your Credit and Maintain a Strong Credit Score 2

Small Balance Dings Dr. Howard's Credit 4

Create a Budget... 4

Maintain Adequate Cash Reserves... 5

Set Goals 5

Dr. Daley Buys a Car.. 7

Chapter Two: Student Loans... 9

Keep Excellent Records... 10

Understand Your Loans... 11

Defer Your Loans 12

Consolidate Your Loans 12

Consolidation Crisis.. 18

Chapter Three: Disability Insurance 19

Don't Rely on Social Security Disability Benefits....................... 21

Understand the Features and Benefits of a
Disability Insurance Plan 22

Dr. Muresh Chooses Cost over Benefits.. 26

Check Insurers' Ratings 27

Buy Adequate Disability Insurance Coverage 27

Young, Single Physician Thinks She Doesn't Need Disability

Insurance 29

Chapter Four: Life Insurance 31

Know Your Needs 32

Know the Options 33

Know the Features and Benefits 37

Find a Company with Strong Ratings 39

Choose Your Policy 39

Monitor and Adjust 40

Waiting to Buy, Waiting to Late 40

Chapter Five: Investment Strategies 43

Understand Diversification 44

Know Your Investments 45

Understand Asset Allocation 46

Understand How Asset Classes React with Each Other 50

Establish a Relationship with an Investment Advisor 50

Develop an Exit Strategy 51

Chapter Six : Tax Planning 53

Develop a Relationship with a Professional Advisor 54

Fill Your Buckets 55

Know Your Pre-Retirement Tax Control Options...................... 56

Know Your Tax Shelter Options for Retirement 59

Chapter Seven: Retirement 61

Review the Tax Buckets... 62

Start Now.. 63

Create Your Plan 64

Fund a Roth IRA 65

Max-out Your 401(k), 403(b), or 457 Plan 66

Create A Simplified Employee Pension (SEP) Plan 67

Open a Roth IRA... 67

Start Saving Now, Automatically 67

Explore Annuities and Municipal Bonds 68

Find More Money to Contribute 69

Don't Touch It 70

Evaluate your Plan and Adjust 70

Chapter Eight: Asset Protection.. 73

Build Rapport with Patients to Help Avoid Lawsuits 75

Purchase Adequate Insurance.. 76

Act Early and Get Professional Advice 79

Dr. Tyson Protects Her Assets too Late in the Game...................... 80

Max-Out Your Retirement Accounts... 80

Purchase Annuities and Life Insurance (Some States).............. 80

Title Property Correctly 81

Gift Your Assets 82

Transfer Your Assets to a Family Limited Partnership 82

Use Business Entities to Shelter Assets 83

Create Trusts 83

Protect Your Accounts Receivable 84

Chapter Nine: Estate Planning 85

Build a Team 86

Prepare Estate Planning Documents and Keep
    Them Current 86

Avoid Probate 87

Shelter Your Estate from Taxes 88

Chapter Ten: Negotiating Your Contract 91

Understand the Terms of a Contract 92

Follow the Negotiation Timeline 104

Final Thoughts 109

Introduction

Residency can be a difficult and frustrating experience. The first year brings questions: Will I be a successful doctor? What will I accomplish? Do I have what it takes to survive? As your training progresses, you develop a fund of knowledge and the medical experience to fully prepare yourself for your medical practice. As you near the end of your training, you realize that while your medical expertise has exploded, your business and financial acumen lag behind that of your friends in other professions. You may realize that not only are you ill-prepared to manage your personal finances, but you know very little about the business of medicine. You may have heard colleagues discussing financial strategies that are specific to physicians, and you worry that you know nothing about them. You may carry significant debt and fear that, as a physician, you are a likely target for litigation. In the current climate, getting sued is no longer a question of "if," but "when."

If physicians have the proper tools, information, and strategies in place early in their residencies and fellowships, they can manage their debt, maximize their earning potential, grow their assets, and protect them as much as possible from judgments. We've written Financial Fund of Knowledge to help meet these goals. As financial planners specializing in meeting the unique needs of physicians, we know that we serve our clients best by beginning our work early in their careers.

The time to protect your assets is not after you've accumulated them, but as you start the process of wealth accumulation at the beginning of your career. Years of medical school training are wasted if a physician is injured or becomes ill and is no longer able to work in his chosen field. Proper financial planning protects your greatest asset as a physician: your ability to earn money.

We understand the needs of residents, not only as professionals, but because we are family members of successful physicians. We've heard numerous stories of other physicians whose failure to plan, or whose lack of access to the right information, brought a halt to bright careers and caused wealth to elude them.

Financial Fund of Knowledge provides doctors an overview of the information needed to help them meet their financial goals by planning early during their residencies. We do not intend for this guide to be an exhaustive resource. We've kept the book to a reasonable length to make it user friendly and to help you take the next step.

Each chapter begins with an overview and includes a list of tools and a recommended strategy for meeting each goal. We include tips and missteps at the end of many chapters to help you make the most of the chapter information. To help illustrate the points in some chapters, we have sprinkled in a few anecdotes.

Additional resources are listed in the book to point you in the right direction for each topic. If you haven't already done so, choosing a team of advisors early makes sense. Ask for references from your medical school, employer, or colleagues. Many advisors offer complimentary initial consultations, allowing you the opportunity to determine if their goals and experience align with yours. Establishing these relationships early in your career will help you reach your financial goals and protect your ability to earn.

The anecdotes in the book illustrate the strategies we recommend to our clients. Some may apply to your circumstances while others may not. Investing and financial planning are very individualized endeavors, and we urge you to take anything you learn from this guide to your advisors before initiating any changes in your finances.

This will provide confirmation that what sounded right for you in a scenario in the guide is indeed the right move.

Financial planning books abound. Financial Fund of Knowledge is different because it addresses the specific needs of doctors with a special emphasis on residents and fellows. We're uniquely qualified to give you this advice because our financial planning practices cater to the needs and interests of doctors. Michael Reiman is President of Reiman Financial, LLC in Dallas, Texas. Max Adams is President of M.A. Financial Group in Miami, Florida. Reiman Financial, LLC and M.A. Financial Group are names that thousands of doctors have trusted as partners in their financial planning process.

No doubt there are many well-qualified individuals who could give you sound financial advice; however, we pride ourselves on understanding the physician's litigation risks, training and career options, wealth patterns, student loans, and other specifics of physicians' financial situations. Financial Fund of Knowledge brings our fund of knowledge to doctors who understand that medicine is a business and who need to enhance their business and financial fund of knowledge. We help physicians make decisions based on the specific risks and rewards of their occupation and their unique situations.

Every physician's needs are different. Area of practice, specialty, size of loans, marital status, number of dependents, risk tolerance, and long and short-term goals are all factors that a financial planner considers when helping you create your financial road map. We hope that after reading this book, you'll recognize how much financial power a qualified professional can give you. If you don't have a financial planner who specializes in physicians' needs, make finding one your first step. If you already have a planner, we hope that you'll be able to make better use of that partnership after reading Financial Fund of Knowledge.

If you have questions about your financial needs, we'd love to hear from you. Drop in on our websites at www.reimanfinancial.

com or www.mafinancialgroup.com for more helpful financial information and planning tools.

As you begin your journey to the successful career that you've worked so hard to achieve, we wish you the best of luck. For more information about the services we provide to our clients, please contact Michael at michaelreiman@reimanfinancial.com or by phone at 214-866-0707 or Max at mafinancial@bellsouth.net or by phone at 305-887-9060.

Michael Reiman, CFS, RFC, DIA
Max Adams, Esq., LUTCF, CRFA

Chapter One

The Personal Money Management Strategy

The Personal Money Management Strategy provides a strong foundation for your financial health.

Goal

Maintain adequate cash reserves and manage your budget to properly maximize your earnings.

The foundation for your financial success involves several basic steps. Many of our clients know the importance of the personal money management strategy but fail to implement it. The result usually involves making decisions that create a financial pinch and/or wasting funds that could be put to better use.

Tools

- Organized Filing System
- Strong Credit Rating
- Budget
- Long and Short Term Goals

Strategy

Stay Organized

It may be difficult to keep up with your mail and bills while work-ing and studying day and night. However, you should set aside a regular time in your schedule each week to review your mail and pay your bills. Notices about the status of your student loans must be read and filed in a timely manner. Your student loan files help you determine if you can defer and whether or not consolidation is right for you. (We discuss student loans in greater detail in Chapter Two.) Additionally, paying your bills on time protects your credit rating, which is an important part of the Personal Money Management Strategy.

Protect Your Credit and Maintain a Strong Credit Score

During and after your residency, you will need to access credit for a variety of reasons. You may decide to purchase a car or home. You may choose to buy-into a practice. These decisions will necessitate a strong credit rating. Some employers request copies of your credit report, and your credit history may affect your employment offers or partnership agreements.

Lenders rate a potential borrower's creditworthiness with a credit score. Credit scores are known as FICO, Beacon, or Empirica scores depending upon which agency prepares the score. Lenders consider this source a reliable means of determining a borrower's ability to repay debt. A strong credit score makes obtaining loans easier and may also lead to lower interest rates on loans.

To keep your credit strong and your scores high, you need to:

   • Establish a credit history. Open a credit card account,

and pay your bills on time. Lack of a credit history can result in a lower score.

- Pay down your credit card balances. A large outstanding balance on a credit account reduces your score.
- Limit credit applications. Applying for credit too frequently can lead to score reductions.
- Fix errors on your credit report.
- Pay your bills on time.
- Close out any unused lines of credit with zero balances. Request a letter from the credit card company confirming that the account has been closed. Cut up the card. Keep a copy of the letter with your credit report file.
- Request a copy of your credit report every one to two years from one of the three credit reporting bureaus:

    www.experian.com

    www.equifax.com

    www.transunion.com

You've probably heard that credit reports are prone to errors. This is especially important for residents to consider. With numerous student loans on your credit history, you may be more likely than others to have mistakes on your report. Check all reported student loans against the records in your file.

After September 1, 2005, you may request one copy of your credit report each year from the reporting agencies. (The law mandating this went into effect in selected states in December 2004, and continues to be phased in until all states are covered.) If an institution denies you credit, you are entitled to a free copy of your report within sixty days of receipt of the company's decision.

If you find any mistakes in your report, contact the credit bureau to make the necessary changes and document your communications with the credit bureau. Identity theft is becoming more common, so check for evidence of fraudulent activity and take steps to get it off your credit report. After the report is cleaned up, request a copy of the accurate report for your records.

Small Balance Dings Dr. Howard's Credit

Dr. Howard started his first practice with two colleagues. The young doctors needed a phone line quickly, and Dr. Howard agreed to put the phone in his name. When the account was finally closed, a small balance remained on the account. Dr. Howard forgot about the account and failed to settle the small balance. The phone company did not forget about the amount owed. The small balance was reported to a collection agency. Thirty years later when Dr. Howard attempted to refinance his home, his credit report indicated a charged-off account, and Dr. Howard's credit score reflected the forgotten incident.

Create a Budget

Many people find a budget to be a nuisance. Creating a budget, however, allows you to determine how much money you have available for building your reserve and investing. A budget will also identify any cash flow problems that may need to be corrected.

To create your budget, list your monthly expenditures for discretionary and fixed expenses. Fixed expenses are those which must be paid monthly without adjustment such as loans, mortgage/rent, insurance, auto payments, and food. Discretionary expenses include categories that could be adjusted, such as entertainment, dining, and travel.

Determine your budget by calculating your net monthly income (income after taxes) and then subtracting the two expense figures. Any surplus can be directed toward additional investments (See

Chapter Five) or increased insurance coverage (Chapters Three and Four). If your budget results in a deficit, revisit your spending categories to find areas in which you may be able to trim spending or possibly consider moonlighting.

Although creating a budget can be an unpleasant task, a budget is a useful tool. Record your actual expenses for several months to compare to your budget. This exercise will help you maintain your saving and spending goals.

Maintain Adequate Cash Reserves

After years without income, you may be tempted to start spending once you begin your residency. Before making purchases, make contributions to a cash reserve account. Your goal should be to build-up a reserve equivalent to three to six months' worth of your committed expenses. To build your reserve, set aside a predetermined amount each month until you reach your goal. Try to start contributing ten percent of your earnings to a cash reserve account. If you can't contribute ten percent, start at some level even if it means you have to increase your contribution amount from time to time. Once you've met your cash reserve goal, you'll be in the habit of paying yourself. Continue to contribute ten percent (or your designated amount), but deposit the money into a different investment vehicle. (We'll discuss these options in Chapter Five.) Without a reserve, a minor emergency can send you into a financial tailspin that may contribute to serious financial consequences. Keep your cash reserves in safe, liquid accounts such as money market accounts, savings accounts, or similar instruments.

Set Goals

Financial planning involves setting goals, drafting a plan to reach those goals and monitoring your progress toward those goals. Set your long and short term goals now so that as you move through your residency and begin your career, you'll make choices that help you provide for your goals. For example, many physicians purchase their first home during residency. If this is a goal for you, you'll know to adjust your spending and savings to account for this. Plus, after you hit your reserve goals, additional deposits of the same amount can be directed toward an account or investment vehicle designated for your down payment savings.

Which investment vehicles best suit your needs? If you plan to buy a home during your residency, Certificates of Deposit (CDs) may be better suited than money market and passbook savings accounts. If you're buying a house in the next six months, your best option is usually to hold the money in your bank account, depending upon current interest rates. Otherwise, a laddered CD strategy is a good place for your down payment. Your financial planner will help you determine the best vehicles for your goals based on current interest rates.

Many of our clients choose to ladder CDs with money earmarked for a series of mid-range goals, such as a down payment on a home or buying into a practice. Instead of purchasing one large CD, these clients use the same amount of money to purchase smaller CDs with different terms. When laddering CDs, you have access to cash more frequently than if you had purchased one longer-term CD. Plus you can take advantage of some rising interest rates that may occur while your money is invested in the CD. For example, with $5,000 to deposit in a safe, liquid account, you could purchase one five-year CD. If you need to access your money during that period, you will incur early withdrawal penalties. By laddering the deposit, you can have access to a portion of the cash at more frequent intervals.

Here's how laddering works. You'll invest the $5,000 in separate CDs of varying terms. For example, you can buy a series of CDs with different terms: three, six, nine, twelve, and fifteen months. You fund each account with a $1,000 initial deposit. In three months, your first rung CD matures. You reinvest the money and earnings from that CD into the fifteen month CD. Then, every other CD moves up one rung. Under this scenario, you have access to some of your cash every three months; you have the potential to earn more than the one long term CD if rates rise during the next five years. You can build a laddered CD portfolio that's aggressive — offering access to smaller amounts less frequently - or one that's more conservative — offering access to the most money most frequently. Your financial planner can help you choose the laddered portfolio that works best for your goals. For a laddered CD builder and calculator, visit www.bankrate.com.

The Personal Money Management Strategy is the first step to building a sound financial base. Once your base is constructed, you're ready to focus your financial energy on protecting and accumulating wealth.

Dr. Daley Buys a Car

Dr. Daley was in his second year of residency, with no cash reserve, no investment plan, and a tremendous amount of debt. Once he began receiving a paycheck, he bought himself a small amount of furniture, a nice television, and some athletic equipment as a reward for completing medical school. He had several credit card accounts with balances, but he used offers for low interest rate credit card balance transfers to keep reducing his minimum monthly payments. When his car's transmission dropped, Dr. Daley decided he would be better off buying a new vehicle. Although he had no concerns about his creditworthiness, Dr. Daley was astonished when the finance manager explained that his credit score was too low to qualify for the advertised low finance rates. Because of Dr. Daley's multiple credit accounts (many of them new) and his outstanding debt combined with a modest income, his ability to borrow money was impaired.

Chapter Two

Student Loans

Large amounts of debt from student loans can be managed to improve payment options and lower interest rates.

Goal

To utilize student loan payment options and loan consolidation for:

- lowest rates
- most favorable terms
- easier overall management

Years of specialized training allow physicians to command larger than average salaries. That ability comes at a huge cost. According to the American Medical Student Association, the average medical student in the United States accrued more than $104,000 in student debt in 2002. More than 20% of newly graduated physicians reported debt totaling more than $150,000.[1] Making the right decisions about student loans allows physicians to make the most of their hard earned salaries while shaving off thousands of dollars over the life

---

1 " Medical Student Debt." AMSA.org. The American Medical Student Association's Legislative Action Center. 27 Jan. 2005. www.amsa.org/legislativecenter/.

of the loans. Like most topics in this book, knowledge and a sound strategy will pay big dividends.

Tools

Student Loan Contact Log, File, and Calendar

Deferment and Forbearance Options

Consolidation

Strategy

Keep Excellent Records

We've already discussed the importance of keeping your financial files organized. This is critical with student loan documents. Loan servicers typically buy and sell notes multiple times during the life of a loan. These frequent changes can lead to confusion. Keep a separate file for each loan. Put every correspondence regarding the loan in the file.

It is also a good idea to maintain a contact log in each file. Any time you speak to someone regarding any of your loans, make a note of the contact person's name, phone number or email address, and the date. Summarize what you discussed and the proposed outcome by the contact person. If the contact person agreed to get back to you, make a note of the follow-up date. You should initiate follow-up contact, if you haven't heard from your contact person or received the desired outcome by the due date.

A final helpful tool for residents to manage student loans is a loan calendar. Create a calendar that lists dates for forbearance and deferment forms and all deadlines pertaining to your loans. Be sure to keep copies of every form you file.

Understand Your Loans

To make the best decisions about your loan, you'll need to understand all of the loan terms. This will allow you to understand the options for managing the loans, while weighing the benefits of each option.

Student loans offer a range of repayment options. The goal for choosing a repayment option is always to get the most flexibility for the least expense. The four repayment options for Direct and Federal Family Education Loans (FFEL) are:

Standard

Standard repayments offer fixed monthly payments for a period of up to ten years, excluding any deferment and forbearance options.

Extended

Extended plans also offer fixed monthly payments over a twelve to thirty-year payment period. Extended plans offer lower monthly payments but higher interest rates.

Income Sensitive (FFEL) or Income Contingent (Direct Loans)

These options allow monthly payment amounts dependent upon income and loan amount. The income contingent payment schedule also allows for lower monthly payments but higher interest rates based on yearly income, family size, interest rate, and loan amount.

Graduated

These plans offer lower payments at first with gradually increasing monthly payment amounts. The payment amounts usually increase every two years.

Every student loan offers a grace period that allows you time to transition from finishing school to entering repayment. Most loans offer a six-month grace period; you can also apply for deferment

11

or forbearance. Deferment is a period of time in which payments are temporarily suspended. During deferment, no interest accrues. Deferments must be requested and approved; they are not automatic. Deferments may be requested when you are experiencing periods of economic hardship or while you are enrolled in an approved graduate fellowship program.

If you are not eligible for deferment, but you temporarily can't make your payments, you may apply for forbearance. Forbearance is granted for limited and specific periods. During forbearance, payments may be suspended or reduced for twelve-month intervals. Forbearance may be granted for a total of up to three years. Interest accrues during forbearance. Like deferment, forbearance is not automatic. You must apply for and be granted forbearance. To determine your deferment and forbearance options, contact the lender or agency that holds your loan.

You should be aware of the guidelines for accessing these options. For example, many physicians take advantage of moonlighting as a way of supplementing their income during residency. Additional income earned during residency may make you ineligible for deferment. Knowing the guidelines for these options allows you to maximize their power.

Many residents use loan consolidation to reduce interest rates or to increase cash flow by reducing their monthly payment. Under consolidation, multiple loans are refinanced. The original loan's provisions (including all grace, deferment, and forbearance options) usually terminate when the original note is consolidated. Most federal student loans are eligible for consolidation, but, by law, private and federal loans cannot be consolidated together. You can generally consolidate during grace, deferment, forbearance, or repayment. Verify your options with your loan agency or servicer.

Defer Your Loans

Deferment can be a useful tool for managing your student loans. Your financial advisor will help you determine when deferment is advantageous and the best time to request deferment. As previously mentioned, keep copies of all forms filed and continue to make payments while your request for deferment is being processed. Missed payments could cause your loan to enter default.

Consolidate Your Loans

Perhaps one of the best decisions you can make is to consolidate your student loans. Consolidation could yield lower monthly payments and lower interest rates. You also benefit from the convenience of one monthly payment. The decision to consolidate is an individual one that should be judged by your unique circumstances. Consolidation may not be advantageous in your situation. We strongly advise you to consult a financial advisor who specializes in physicians' needs before making the decision to consolidate.

Under consolidation, all provisions of the old loan, including deferment options, are lost. After the consolidation, you'll be bound to the provisions of the new loan consolidation. As a result, you should carefully consider, with the advice of your advisors, whether you are better served under the terms of your current loan or a new loan.

Several consolidation options exist. To determine your FFEL consolidation options, contact your lender. If your loans are Direct Loans, you can obtain consolidation details from the Loan Origination Center's Federal Direct Consolidation Loans Information Center at the Department of Education online at www.loanconsolidation.ed.gov or www.dl.ed.gov.

In many cases, consolidation makes sense for residents and can result in saving thousands of dollars over the life of the loan. With interest rates still near historic lows, we have recently seen opportunities to refinance student loans at fixed rates as low as 3.5%.

Work with your financial advisor to time the consolidation of your loans for maximum benefit. The best time to consolidate depends upon your circumstances and the loan types. For example, if you are nearing the end of your residency and are close to an increase in income, you may not need to take advantage of your deferments and might benefit from consolidation now. By contrast, if you are entering a lengthy residency, you may be better served by using all of your current deferment options before consolidation.

The timing of your consolidation may reduce your rates. Variable Stafford rates change every year on July 1. The new rate is usually announced approximately a month in advance. You can check the new rate in June to determine if you would reduce your loan costs by consolidating before the rate change or if you would be better served by waiting. Be sure to discuss other timing issues with your financial advisor to determine when to initiate consolidation.

Residents facing cash flow problems may be able to free up additional money by consolidating current loans into (possibly) lower rate loans with more flexible payment terms. For the greatest reduction in your monthly payment, you can choose an extended payment schedule. Of course, over the life of the loan, your repayment amount is higher, but your financial advisor can work with you to create a repayment schedule utilizing additional payments, which will lower the cost of interest paid.

To consolidate your loans, start by contacting the organization that services your student loans or the institutions that own the loans. For information regarding student loan consolidation, visit the Direct Loan Servicing Center at www.dl.ed.gov, www.salliemae. com, or www.loanconsolidation.ed.gov. For consolidation of private loans, see www.studentloans.com.

When making the decision about consolidation, you'll need to consider all terms of the note, not simply the interest rate. Some topics you'll want to explore with the consolidation company and your financial advisor are:

Interest Rate

Get the interest rate for the consolidation loan; if the rate is variable, request information on the interest rate cap.

Monthly Payment/Repayment Schedule

Know the amount you will be expected to pay on the new loan. Explore flexible repayment schedules, such as income contingent, graduated, or extended.

Total Repayment Amount

How much will the loan cost you? When the loan is repaid, what is the total cost?

Hidden Fees and Charges

There should be no charge to consolidate your student loans, but you should be aware of the costs associated with increased interest from an extended repayment plan. You'll also need to be aware of the effects of capitalization on your decision. Most unsubsidized loans capitalize accrued and unpaid interest at the time you repay your loan. Capitalizing interest is a process in which the lender charges the borrower for all interest that has accrued plus all unpaid interest on the balance of the loan. Capitalized interest can add significantly to the cost of consolidation. If you consolidate this type of loan, you'll pay accrued and unpaid interest at the time of consolidation. This cost should be factored into your decision.

Grace, Deferment, Forbearance

Find out how consolidation impacts these provisions. As a result of consolidation, you'll generally lose or gain deferments. In most cases, the grace, deferment, and forbearance options on your current loan cease to exist once you consolidate your loan. One exception is the HEAL refinance option, which allows current provisions of grace, deferment, and forbearance to stay in place.

Interest Subsidy

The federal government pays the interest on a subsidized student loan. The interest is subsidized while the borrower is in school and during the grace period. Determine how the consolidation will impact your subsidized loans. Will you lose the subsidy if you consolidate?

Early Payment Penalty

Most consolidation loans do not have this provision, but you want to be certain before you make any decisions about a new loan. Be sure to find out how the servicer applies additional payments to the loan.

Repayment Incentives

Some loans offer repayment incentives that can reduce your interest rates. These include on-time incentives, which drop rates after a specified number of on-time payments, and rate reductions for paying for your loan through automatic withdrawals (EFT) from your bank account.

Cancellation

Most student loans are cancelled if the borrower becomes disabled or dies.

Servicer

Determine who will service the new loan and what happens to the loan servicer if the note is sold by the lender. It is not unusual for a student loan to be bought and sold several times over the course of the repayment period.

Processing Time

It may take up to two months to process your new loan. You'll need to know the status of any loans in grace, deferment, or forbearance during this time. Continue to make payments on your current loan during the application process. Missing payments could send your loan into default.

You have several options for managing repayment of your student loans. We strongly recommend that you execute your due diligence with your loan options. Your financial advisor can help you determine the relative costs of current and new loans based on the information you receive from the lender or servicer. Knowledge is not only power when it comes to student loans, but it is also money in the bank.

Tip

Understand how interest is capitalized on your current loan. Your loan servicer should explain when interest is capitalized. The interest on your note can be added to the principal before, during, or after deferment or forbearance and will be rolled into the new note at the time of consolidation, increasing the amount of principal of the new loan.

Misstep

Some physicians may consider consolidating student loans with their spouse, who is also a physician. Discuss this option very carefully with your financial advisor. Most student loans are forgiven if the borrower dies or becomes disabled. Under a consolidated loan for both spouses, the entire amount would most likely still be due in the case of death or disability of one spouse. This could cause an unnecessary strain on the surviving spouse. If the notes are instead kept separate, the balance of the deceased spouse's loan will be forgiven, freeing the surviving spouse from the obligation. Plus, in the case of separation or divorce, both parties are considered jointly liable for repayment of the loan. Regardless of original individual loan size, after a divorce, both parties would be responsible for shared portions of the new notes.

Consolidation Crisis

Dr. Latko's medical student loans amounted to a large portion of his debt. His wife Laura, who was a teacher, also had student loans, although they were much smaller than his. During Dr. Latko's residency, he and Laura decided to consolidate their student loans in order to reduce their monthly payment. They both agreed that having one monthly student loan payment would also make things easier for them.

Unfortunately, Dr. Latko was killed in an automobile accident. Laura tried to move forward with her life assuming responsibility for the financial affairs of the estate. She was shocked to learn that, even after her husband's death, she would be required to continue to pay off his student loan obligations. She and her husband had believed that the loan would be forgiven if one of them died. They did not realize that the decision to consolidate years earlier would make Laura responsible for Dr. Latko's medical school loans, if he died. Because the Latkos did not anticipate this situation, they did not purchase enough life insurance to cover the cost of the student loan obligation. Laura was forced to sell off assets from the estate in order to satisfy her deceased husband's student loan obligations.

Chapter Three

Disability Insurance

You are much more likely to become disabled than to die during your working years. Purchasing ample disability insurance protects your greatest asset: your ability to earn money.

Goal

Purchase the amount of disability coverage you can afford now. Budget disability insurance premiums as a committed expense.

If your three most valuable assets were worth $20,000, $200,000, and $2,000,000, which one would you choose to insure? In theory, it's a no-brainer, right? However, in practice, the majority of individuals don't make the obvious choice. Not convinced? How many people insure the value of their automobiles? Most everyone. The same applies for individuals who own $200,000 homes. Insurance is required by lenders, so most people insure their homes. How many of those same people insure their greatest asset, their potential to earn money? Very few.

Yet statistics show that you are more likely to become disabled than to die in your working years. According to research compiled by E F Moody, a 40 year-old stands a 64% chance of becoming disabled for 90 days or more before reaching age 65. Moody also notes that according to the Society of Actuaries, more people remain disabled than die or recover five years after the onset of the disability, illness, or injury. In a study of individuals who became ill or disabled at age 45, 21.5% had recovered after five years, and 19.9% died from the illness or injury. The remaining 58.6% were still disabled after five years, and as the quality of medical treatments continues to improve, individuals with disabilities will live longer. When you consider that less than 60% of working Americans have any type of disability coverage, you can understand why the Department of Housing and Urban Development reports that one-half of all mortgage foreclosures are a result of a disabling condition (sixteen times the number of foreclosures resulting from death).[2]

If you became disabled tomorrow, could you continue to pay off your debts, meet your financial obligations, provide for your family, and maintain your lifestyle? The fact is that, after a disability, when your income is greatly reduced, your expenses are likely to skyrocket. Disability insurance is a critical and too often overlooked component of a physician's financial plan. It is no accident that we placed the discussion of disability insurance early in this book. Buying a stock or a mutual fund may seem more exciting than purchasing a disability policy, but what good is accumulating wealth if you can't protect it? Adequate disability coverage combined with life insurance acts like pillars that support and maintain your accumulated wealth. Without the support of disability insurance, your assets could crumble after one unfortunate event.

---

2 Moody, Errold F, Jr. "Disability Probability." Efmoody.com. 15 Dec 2004 http://www.efmoody.com/insurance/disabilitystatistics.html

Tools

Individual Disability Insurance Policy

Strategy

Don't Rely on Social Security Disability Benefits

Social Security provides disability payments under certain conditions. The Social Security Administration's definition of disability is too narrow to be of real value in planning for your financial needs after a disability. Under Social Security guidelines, you are considered disabled if "you cannot do work that you did before", and the SSA determines that "you cannot adjust to other work because of your medical condition(s). Your disability must also last or be expected to last for at least one year or to result in death." That's pretty broad. In addition, many Social Security disability claims are denied.

In most cases, Social Security Disability Income (SSDI) will not protect you in case of disability. At best it will provide a little extra income. You can check how much your SSDI benefits are worth by reviewing your Social Security benefits statement. If you haven't received one in the last three years, visit www.ssa.gov to request a copy. The Social Security Administration's website also provides a benefits calculator that you can use to verify how little you can expect from an income protection plan built upon Social Security Disability benefits.

Understand the Features and Benefits of a Disability Insurance Plan

The second worst thing that could probably happen to you is that you could become disabled without coverage. What's worse than that? Buying a disability plan, becoming disabled, and then learning that your claim is denied because of exclusions or terms in your disability contract. Even though you spent thousands of dollars paying for a policy that you thought would protect you, you're now in the same boat as someone without any coverage, minus the valuable dollars you wasted on a policy that doesn't serve your needs. You can avoid this worst case scenario by understanding the terms in your contract before you purchase.

Familiarize yourself with the features and benefits available through a disability insurance policy to help you choose the coverage that is best for you. Every disability insurance contract is different, and contracts can vary widely. Surgeons, for example, are in a different insurance class than dermatologists or radiologists. Some classes won't be eligible for some features. The provisions of your contract depend upon your specialty, as well as other factors unique to your situation.

One of the most important steps to choosing a policy is understanding exactly what you are buying. A disability insurance policy pays you a monthly benefit if you become disabled from an illness or injury for most reasons, depending upon what your contract defines as a disability and the exclusions of your contract. Exclusions might include: mental/nervous disorder, war, self-inflicted injuries, residing in a foreign country, and incarceration.

When you purchase a policy, you will be receiving coverage for a specific monthly benefit amount. Your goal in choosing a disability insurance policy is locating the most comprehensive protection available. Following are some of the most important features to consider when choosing a disability policy:

A Total Disability policy requires that you become totally disabled before it pays benefits. Your contract should include a specific definition of disability. Disability policies can be determined in two ways: "own-occupation" or "any occupation". Perhaps the most important feature of a physician's disability insurance policy is an "own-occupation" (or "own-occ") designation. The way your policy defines disability will determine whether or not the benefit will pay if you can go back to work in a different occupation (if you choose to) after your disability or illness. This could mean the difference between tens of thousands of dollars in earned income and benefits paid, so pay close attention to your policy's language.

A policy with an Own-Occupation designation provides benefits if you become disabled and cannot perform in your specific occupation, usually the one you were engaged in at the time of the disability. This applies even if you continue to work in a related area in your field, such as teaching medical school or switching to general practice. Any Occupation policies (or general occupation policies) are much more restrictive and will not pay a benefit if, after the illness or injury, you are able to work at any job for which you are reasonably suited. Consider how this difference would impact a surgeon who develops carpal tunnel syndrome and is unable to practice surgery. She could still teach or find other related employment, and under an own-occupation policy, she would also receive a monthly benefit to supplement her income. Under an any-occupation policy, this same doctor would receive no benefits if she is able to work at anything for which she is reasonably trained, thus not meeting the definition for disability. An own-occupation policy will cost more, but the added protection afforded by this type of coverage is worth the extra expense.

Review your proposed insurance contract carefully. Some companies offer a policy that's actually a modified own-occ. A true own-occ policy will clearly define your occupation. Although these policies were once relatively easy to obtain, disability insurance policies for physicians have become less comprehensive. Check the length of the terms, as well. Own-occ policies that pay benefits to age 65 are becoming a rarity. Most own-occ policies pay benefits for only two or five years. Currently only a handful of insurance companies underwrite comprehensive individual disability polices for physicians.

Renewability is an important provision of your disability insurance policy. Under guaranteed renewable policies, the provisions remain unchanged, but the premium can be increased. Non-cancelable and guaranteed renewable plans maintain the original provisions; Plus, the premiums stay the same. As long as you pay the premium, the policy cannot be changed or cancelled by the insurer.

Residual Disability feature will pay a proportional benefit according to how the disability impacts your ability to work and your income. As long as the illness or injury prevents full-time work, you can receive a portion of the benefit, usually the portion of income you lost. The portion that allows you to claim disability varies in most contracts. The method for calculating benefits varies from insurer to insurer. Some contracts will look at the last month, and others will average the last six months of income.

A Recovery Benefit allows you to rebuild your income after you recover from the illness or injury and return to work. If you have experienced lost income, this benefit will pay once you return to work.

As a resident, you may be particularly interested in Future Insurability. This feature allows you to increase your coverage without requiring medical underwriting. This option is beneficial for residents as it allows you to increase your benefit amount as your income rises. When you exercise a Future Insurability policy, it is subject to financial underwriting. Each contract specifies when this option can be exercised. Some contracts cap the benefit amount each year. Some only allow you to exercise the option while

24

you are disabled, and others will allow you to exercise the option when you are not disabled. All disability insurance policies have an Elimination (waiting) Period. The elimination period determines the amount of time between the injury or illness and the payment of benefits on a claim (usually 60 – 180 days).

Lifetime Benefit provisions are becoming rare. Many policies stop providing at age 65. Normal life expectancy extends well beyond 65. If you were to become disabled early in your career and live to your life expectancy, you'd be without benefits for many years without a lifetime benefit on your policy.

Note whether your proposed contract includes a Cost of Living Rider. A Cost of Living Rider protect your benefits from inflation. If you incur a disability, the rider allows adjustments to your monthly benefits payments to keep up with inflation. Adjustments are generally tied to the Consumer Price Index and have a maximum yearly adjustment. Total Cost of Living adjustments may be capped under some policies and usually come into effect at disability.

A Presumptive Disability feature recognizes you as totally disabled under certain situations such as complete loss of sight, hearing, speech, use of both legs or arms, or use of both one arm and one leg.

Policies with a Capital Sum Benefit offer a lump sum amount (typically your monthly benefit times a range of five to twelve). You are eligible for the lump sum benefit for other losses defined in your contract. Common losses eligible for this benefit include a severed hand or foot or total loss of eyesight in one eye.

Plans with a Social Security Benefit add an extra payment to the monthly benefit amount if your disability claim is denied by the Social Security Administration. This feature is difficult to obtain because the group policy, offered through employers, usually carries the benefit.

Other features that may be offered on a disability insurance policy include an Automatic Increase Rider, which automatically increases your benefits amount to match your rising income level. Premium Waivers allow you to suspend premium payments if you become disabled. Some plans offer Rehabilitation Benefits that pay a portion of the expenses incurred while you're enrolled in rehabilitation. Transplant and Cosmetic Surgery benefits are also built into some contracts.

Many policies limit claims on some existing conditions such as mental/nervous disorder and substance abuse. Exclusions may also include chronic pain, fibromyalgia, and chronic fatigue syndrome. Check your contract carefully for a complete list of exclusions.

Dr. Muresh Chooses Cost over Benefits

Dr. Muresh purchased disability insurance during his residency. He didn't really want all the bells and whistles, so he purchased the basics. He knew his decision was a good one because it had resulted in the savings of thousands of dollars compared to the premiums of his colleagues who went for a more expensive plan. Dr. Muresh loved to ski and never missed an opening weekend at his favorite resort. One year he decided to attempt to snowboard, and was injured in a serious accident that severely limited the use of his left arm. Dr. Muresh made a claim on his disability insurance policy and was shocked when the denial letter arrived in the mail. Although Dr. Muresh was unable to continue his medical practice, his insurance carrier claimed that he was still able to find employment in another field and would not pay the claim. Dr. Muresh's partner examined his policy and noticed that, indeed, the policy did not include an own-occupation benefit. Dr. Muresh's mounting medical and rehabilitation costs combined with his lost income forced him to sell his home. Dr. Muresh realized, too late, that purchasing a policy with the right benefits and features would have helped save his home and his wealth.

Check Insurers' Ratings

Before purchasing individual disability coverage, check the financial ratings of the companies you are considering as insurers. Rating services monitor and rate financial services and insurance companies based on analysis of many factors, including annual and quarterly financial statements, reports from State Insurance Commissioners, and information received directly from the insurance companies. Weiss Ratings (www.weissratings.com), A.M. Best (www.ambest.com), and Standard and Poor's (www.standandpoors.com) provide reliable ratings of insurance companies. High ratings indicate a company with financial strength. Choose a company that gets high marks from at least two of these sources.

Buy Adequate Disability Insurance Coverage

Many organizations, physician employers, or groups offer group disability coverage. Many cash strapped residents find purchasing individual disability insurance an unnecessary expense when they are covered on a group plan. A group plan is a start, but, in many cases, it cannot provide adequate coverage. As a matter of fact, group plans often have stricter definitions of disability and more exclusions. Payments from Social Security, Workers Compensation, lump sum settlements, or other types of compensation related to your accident or illness may reduce or cancel out your group benefits. Often these plans can be changed, and premiums can increase at any time. Generally, the coverage limit is lower than the limits available under individual plans. Many group plans offer only sixty percent of your salary with a set maximum benefit amount.

An individual plan is not dependent upon your affiliation with an employer. A group plan, however, protects you only under the employer who offered it. If you leave the employer, your group plan (if it's not portable) will need to be converted to an individual policy.

Whereas individual policies also provide a tax-benefit (because benefits are paid to you tax-free), you are responsible for taxes owed on any benefits paid by the group plan, if your employer pays for the premium and takes it as a business deduction.

You can purchase individual coverage through an insurance company. Your financial advisor may also be able to refer you to brokers and insurance sales agents. Also inquire about special arrangements your employer may have with specific companies. These types of programs may be offered as opt-in benefits in which you are responsible for the premium payment (ensuring that any benefits paid to you are tax-free.) The advantage to such a policy sometimes includes more relaxed underwriting guidelines and significantly discounted rates compared to individual policies.

Remember that every disability contract is different. The best contract for you might not necessarily fit the needs of a colleague. Understand exactly what features and benefits your policy proposes to offer you before you buy. Also, ask your financial advisor or other qualified professional to review all contracts before you commit. Taking the next step in building your financial plan without adequate disability insurance equates to putting a roof on your dream home without the proper pillars to support it. The lack of support is sure to bring the whole thing toppling down.

Tips

Buy an own-occupation policy to age 65 and, if available, purchase a lifetime benefit option.

When purchasing a residual benefit policy, look for an option that pays for the loss of income as opposed to loss of time or duties.

Purchase a plan with future insurability. This will allow you to expand your coverage without providing new medical history. You will want to increase your coverage once you complete your residency and your income increases significantly. As a resident, your maximum benefit amount is limited by insurance companies. The future insurability provision helps you guarantee that your ability to earn will always be adequately protected.

Get a policy with the fewest exclusions possible. Multiple exclusions may lead to inadequate protection.

Young, Single Physician Thinks She Doesn't Need Disability Insurance

Dr. Buckler's huge student loan debt and her modest income were factors in her decision not to purchase disability insurance. Besides, as a single person, she really didn't see the need to protect her income. Her parents were always very supportive of her, and they had the means to help her if anything should happen. She was healthy and young. Disability insurance could wait. Dr. Buckler began having pain in her feet and assumed that the stress from her ER position was exacerbating her overworked and tired feet. The pain worsened, and Dr. Buckler found her long shifts in the ER excruciating. She was soon diagnosed with plantar fasciitis and had to leave her position. She tried to retrain for a job that would not require her to be on her feet as much, but she was unable to get retrained for any other specialties, lacking the money to pay for additional training. Dr. Buckler's assumptions about the need for disability insurance were wrong, but she was correct about her family's support. Unable to maintain her lifestyle, Dr. Buckler moved home to live with her family.

Chapter Four

Life Insurance

Life insurance provides benefits to your dependents after your death and may provide some tax benefits and asset protection (depending on your state).

Goal

Purchase a life insurance policy that will provide enough resources to pay off all existing liabilities and meet the needs of your surviving spouse and/or dependents.

If you were to die today, would your family have the resources for your funeral costs and debt obligations? Would your loved ones have the money to maintain their current lifestyle and to meet future financial needs such as educational expenses for your dependents? Life insurance offers peace of mind for you and your family.

If you die prematurely, life insurance pays a death benefit to your beneficiaries. These tax-free benefits can also be used to pay your estate. Some insurance options provide protection only, while others offer protection plus an investment vehicle. In a policy that offers cash value, you also benefit from tax-deferred accumulation. Some policies also allow you to borrow against the cash value. If managed correctly, some life insurance contracts could be paid out in tax-free dollars.

Tools

Term Life Insurance

Permanent Life Insurance

Whole Life Insurance

Universal Life Insurance

Variable Life Insurance

Strategy

Know Your Needs

To buy true peace of mind, you need to buy the right amount of coverage. The wrong amount will only provide a false sense of security. Purchasing the right amount at the right price is the most important thing about buying life insurance. If you needed $1,000,000 of life insurance, but you bought $500,000 of life insurance, it does not matter what type of policy you have, your beneficiaries are still $500,000 short. As a starting point, to estimate the amount you need, you can find plenty of insurance calculators on the internet, such as the Insurance Estimator at www.reimanfinancial.com or the Lifetime Needs Estimator at www.moneycentral.msn.com/investor/calcs/n_life/main.asp. Your insurance agent or financial advisor can also help you determine a dollar amount to purchase.

Before you can define how much life insurance you need, you must first decide on whether you want to use a needs-based or human life value approach to purchasing insurance. A needs-based approach calculates the amount of insurance needed as the figure equal to the cost to cover funeral arrangements and/or bills or obligations. The human life value approach is based on how much your life is worth financially to your family. It is also an estimation of the dollar amount that will allow your loved ones to maintain their current lifestyle and financial goals if you were to die tomorrow. Once you choose a valuation approach, determining how much life insurance to buy is much easier. You should clarify your goals by asking your spouse these questions:

If I die today, would you want to pay off the mortgage immediately?

Would you want to pay off loans for automobiles and other vehicles?

Would paying off other existing liabilities be a priority?

Would you want to pay off student loans or set-aside money for college expenses for dependents?

Would you want to continue to fund your wealth accumulation accounts?

Would my death lead to additional childcare expenses? If so, for how many years?

Would you seek employment or work more hours after my death?

How much income do you estimate that you could earn?

Would you work beyond your retirement goal or keep the same target retirement age?

The answers to these questions will help you determine how much protection is adequate.

Know the Options

The variety of life insurance products available allows you to choose a policy that best meets your needs and goals, but the number of choices may also make it difficult to choose. In order to make the decision easier, you should understand the options available to you.

Policies are term or permanent. Term policies offer protection for only a temporary specified period of time: 1, 5, 10, 15, 20, 25, or 30 years. These policies provide a death benefit to your beneficiaries, and if the policy holder outlives the term, the policy lapses. You have no cash value in the policy. Permanent insurance, on the other hand, offers protection until the policyholder dies. Insurance companies offer a range of permanent policy choices.

Term insurance affords the highest death benefit for the least expense. With a term insurance policy, you choose the length of coverage, and the premium usually increases as your age increases. Some term policies offer a level premium throughout the life of the policy. If the premium is not paid, the policy will lapse after the grace period.

If you need to ensure a death benefit for dependents at an affordable rate, term insurance may be your best option. If you prefer an insurance policy that will cover you for the rest of your life and which may offer an investment opportunity, asset protection, and tax benefits, permanent policies might be a better choice for you.

There are several types of permanent life insurance available:

Whole Life Insurance

Whole Life plans protect the insured throughout his lifetime. These plans typically offer a fixed, level premium; level death benefit; and guaranteed cash value. Some policies pay dividends (although dividends are not guaranteed); some policies mature. Under the policy maturation, if the insured is still alive at a designated age, the policy pays the insured the face value of the contract.

Whole Life coverage tends to be a good option for physicians seeking permanent insurance protection that offers a wealth accumulation feature. This product is a bundled product, and it can be difficult to see where the money is going. Typically, whole life plans can assist physicians wanting guaranteed coverage for their whole life. Insurance companies offer a range of whole life policy features including optional riders such as paid-up additions or expanded term coverage.

Variable Whole Life

Variable policies afford you a greater degree of control. Variable insurance premiums are used to pay the cost of insurance and fund an underlying market investment with the balance. Variable policies allow you to control the investment that controls the policy. You can choose different variable life options to meet your specific needs and goals.

As the name suggests, variable whole life works like variable and whole life insurance combined. These plans offer a level premium and a guaranteed minimum death benefit. You direct the additional premium dollars into your choice of investment vehicles offered by the plan. Options usually include mutual fund type accounts. A Variable Whole Life policy's cash value grows with the underlying investment, but the cash value of the policy is not guaranteed. In most policies the cash value depends upon the performance of the underlying investments, unless the policyholder purchases a death benefit guarantee. These policies typically offer a guaranteed minimum death benefit as long as you pay the premium. Physicians who want to invest tax-deferred in the market or who want a hedge against inflation are likely to choose Variable Whole Life.

Universal Life

Universal Life plans tend to be more flexible than whole

life policies. Universal policies offer flexible premiums that may be increased, decreased, or skipped depending upon the provisions of your policy. The death benefit may also increase or decrease based on the limits set forth in your policy. You have two options for your death benefit: level (the death benefit stays the same throughout your contract) or increasing (the death benefit equals the policy's face value plus a cash surrender amount). Universal policies pay interest at a guaranteed minimum rate indicated in the contract. If you allow interest to accrue inside your policy account, the cash value of your policy increases.

Universal Life policies also allow access to your cash surrender values by allowing loans or withdrawals against the policy. The policy is regulated by a First-In/First-Out principal. "First In" refers to the after-tax dollars used to purchase the policy. These first-in funds may be withdrawn from the policy without incurring additional taxes. In some policies, once the first-in dollars have all been withdrawn from the policy, the policyholder can take out loans against the policy's value. In some policies, the policyholder receives the loan proceeds tax-free, as well. When the policyholder dies, the death benefit pays back the loans made against the policy.

Variable Universal Life

Variable Universal Life combines the features of Variable Whole Life and Universal Life to create an aggressive insurance investment option. This plan offers the same features as a Universal plan (flexible premiums and death benefits, two death benefit options, and access to cash value) in combination with an underlying investment in a mutual fund type vehicle. Variable Universal Life has a fluctuating cash value tied to the performance of the associated investment.

You may have heard the advice to "buy term and invest the

difference". You can accomplish this with a Universal Life or a Variable Universal Life policy. When you purchase one of these policies, a portion of your premium pays the cost of your insurance protection and the internal costs of your policy (like buying a term policy), and the balance is deposited into investment options limited to those vehicles that are available in the contract (investing the difference). The internal charges in the contract are higher than a term policy, and you need to determine if the costs are higher than the tax benefits. If so, then you might be better off buying a separate term policy and investing the difference in other vehicles. When the tax benefits outweigh the costs, a Universal Life or a Variable Universal Life product not only allows you to accumulate wealth, but also provides for retirement savings as well.

Group Life Insurance Benefits

Many employers offer term group life insurance as an employee benefit. In some cases, your employer will pay the premium, and you have the option of purchasing additional coverage on the same plan. Group life insurance is often not enough. If you explore this option, you'll want to compare rates for additional coverage with rates for individual plans, as individual plans can be expensive depending upon your health. Also, compare features of both policies and the benefits offered to determine if your group plan really protects you adequately. Note that when you leave the employer, you will lose the coverage unless the policy is portable.

Know the Features and Benefits

As with disability insurance policies, life insurance policies offer a variety of features and benefits. Acquaint yourself with these before you buy so that you'll avoid buying too much or too little coverage, or worse, coverage that doesn't meet your goals. While the following list of features and benefits will help you make a more informed decision, you should consult with a financial advisor or an insurance sales representative to ensure that you are buying a policy that meets your needs.

Contract Term

Available terms or lengths of the policy period usually include 1, 2, 5, 10, 15, 20, 25, 30 year terms. If you are purchasing a term policy, you can typically choose from three types of premiums: level, decreasing, or yearly renewable. Level premiums grant coverage for a set period of time with a premium that remains the same. Decreasing premiums provide a smaller benefit as the term ages. Decreasing term is often used to cover a mortgage or other large obligation. Yearly renewable term offers the option to renew at the end of each year without an increase in premiums.

Death Benefit

The amount paid to your beneficiary or beneficiaries upon your death. This benefit can be level or may increase during the term.

Cash Surrender Value

The cash surrender value is the dollar amount the policy is worth if cashed in.

Dividends/Interest

Some policies will pay dividends and interest inside the policy account.

Maturation

This benefit pays the insured if a specified age is attained.

Portability

Allows the policy to stay with you regardless of your employment.

Convertibility

Some contracts provide an option to convert a term policy into a permanent policy. The conversion usually has to be done by a specific age.

Number of Years Premium Is Guaranteed

The premium will not change during this period.

Understand everything in your proposed contract. Ask your financial advisor to review proposed contracts with you.

Find a Company with Strong Ratings

Finding life insurance companies is easy with the prevalence of internet, television, radio and direct mail advertisements. Nevertheless, be certain to check the financial ratings of companies from which you're considering purchasing a policy. As discussed in the previous chapter, A.M. Best, Standard and Poor's, and Weiss Ratings all offer reliable ratings of insurance companies.

Choose Your Policy

As in medicine where two patients may not benefit from the same course of action, physicians' needs are all different. How do you know if you should buy term and invest the difference or buy universal life which purports to do the same thing? Your financial advisor or insurance agent can help you decide which product best meets your goals based on your tax bracket and other factors. For example, a term policy is less expensive than a universal life policy; Plus, universal life includes charges inside the policy. Under a favorable tax situation, the benefits are returned tax-free. Tax-free benefits must outweigh the costs inside the policy to be advantageous. Your financial advisor will help you determine which policy to choose.

Monitor and Adjust

Life insurance is like the other components of your financial road map: what is right for you in your residency may not be advantageous or appropriate in five years when you are a practicing physician. Meet with your financial advisor regularly to review your life insurance contract to make sure that it still meets your goals. When your goals are no longer being met with your current contract, your advisor should be able to guide you toward a better fit.

Waiting to Buy, Waiting to Late

Dr. Gaines was single and decided to hold-off on the purchase of life insurance. Because he had no dependents to support, he felt the monthly premium amount was better used toward additional payments on his student loans. He had decided that he'd wait two more years and then reevaluate the need. One day while working with a patient in the ER, Dr. Gaines pricked himself with a dirty needle and developed Hepatitis C. As soon as he was diagnosed, he made an appointment with a life insurance agent to discuss purchasing a policy. He decided that if he bought the policy before he became ill he would have a better chance at getting coverage. He left the agent's office empty-handed because the agent informed him that he was now non-insurable.

Tips

Watch out for Accidental Death and Dismemberment (AD&D). In order to receive these benefits, your death must occur under very specific circumstances. Review any AD&D provision carefully to understand exactly what the coverage entails.

Group insurance provided by your employer may be portable. You'll more than likely be required to convert the policy to a more expensive cash-value policy, but you can take it with you after you sever your ties with your employer. Although this is usually not the best way to secure life insurance, if you're uninsurable and won't meet the more stringent underwriting guidelines of an individual plan, your financial advisor may encourage you to stick with the covered group plan.

Chapter Five

Investment Strategies

Develop an investment strategy during your residency that will be the start of wealth accumulation goals. When your investments are properly diversified according to your financial goals, your money grows at the rate of return you are expecting and with the appropriate risk level.

Goal

Properly diversify all investments to maximize return and minimize risks.

At this point in your life it may be difficult to imagine money left-over at the end of the month for investing. When you finish your residency, however, and start to realize more of your earning potential, you'll make better decisions about those extra funds if you spend some time now thinking about future investments. If you are fortunate enough to already have your cash reserves in place, and if you continue to deposit and invest a portion of your monthly salary, you definitely need to understand the best approach for balancing your investments.

Tools

Diversification

Asset Allocation

Investment Advisor

Strategy

Understand Diversification

If we hand you one pencil and ask you to break it, you'll have no problem complying. If we then give you a bundle of ten pencils and make the same request, you will not have much success. That's the essence of diversification. If all your money is invested in one blue chip stock and the company falters, all your investment evaporates with the company's failed performance.

Certainly there is a strong relationship between risk and reward. And you're probably aware that, generally, the greater the risk, the larger the potential reward. That is not, however, a license to make bad investment decisions. Proper diversification allows you to invest at the level that matches your risk tolerance while insulating you from the poor performance of only one investment. For example, stocks tend to be more volatile than other investments such as bonds, CDs, and money market funds. Investing in stocks is for more aggressive investors with a higher tolerance for risk. As a resident with plenty of time on your side, you more than likely fall into this category. However, investing in one company's stock, no matter how secure you feel in the decision, can break your portfolio as easily as you can snap one pencil in half. If, instead, you invest in a mutual fund, your money will be combined with a pool of money from other investors (increasing your buying power) and allow you to invest in an array of stocks. Thus, if one company falters, your entire investment doesn't capsize. Instead of holding one pencil, you've got ten.

Dr. Sandoval Rides the Tech Wave, Dr. Helix Wipes Out

Dr. Sandoval's career in medicine had brought him many personal and financial rewards. He seemed to have the golden touch with his investments. In the early 90's, he invested a portion of his funds in tech stocks and watched as his wealth grew immeasurably. When he retired, his estate was significant, and he was pleased to be able to provide for future generations of Sandovals. Dr. Sandoval's buddy, Dr. Helix, had admired his investment savvy and decided to follow his lead. Dr. Helix took all of his investment money and made stock purchases in the tech sector. Although his wife had expressed some concern about his lack of diversification, he soothed her worries with charts plotting enormous gains in his portfolio. Soon, the bubble burst, and Dr. Helix's investment that was once worth millions had shrunk to a tiny puddle of funds. Dr. Helix had two teenage daughters who would enter college in the next three years, and he feared that his bad decision would limit his ability to provide for their education needs.

Know Your Investments

Some investments are straight-forward, like a money-market or a CD. You understand what you are buying when you purchase the investment. Other types of investments, like mutual funds, may not be as straight-forward. Before you purchase shares in a mutual fund, understand exactly what you're buying. You may believe that, because two mutual funds have different names, you're investing in different asset classes, but that may not be the case. The prospectus will tell you how much of a fund is invested in cash, stocks, bonds, and the corresponding asset classes.

Understand Asset Allocation

Your success as an investor depends more than any other factor on maintaining the right asset allocation. Asset allocation is the distribution of your investment into a mix of investment classes based on your risk tolerance and goals. Here are some of the basic asset class categories for stocks and bonds:

Stocks

Growth vs. Value

Stocks are classified under two categories: growth and value. Growth stocks are defined as stocks of companies with above average earnings over several years with an expectation for continued growth. Growth stocks are more expensive and carry more risk than value stocks. They sell at a premium above the company's perceived worth. Value stocks trade at a lower value than the company's perceived worth. A variety of circumstances surrounding the company could cause its stock to be undervalued, including changes in management, increased costs for raw materials, or poor investments by the company. Often a company's stock can be classified as value simply because of market conditions. Your portfolio should have a mix of value and growth stocks.

Market Capitalization

Inside each stock asset class are three more distinctions regarding the company's market capitalization: large-cap, mid-cap, and small-cap. Market capitalization is determined by multiplying the number of outstanding shares by the stock's market price. Market capitalization distinctions can change over time. The distinction used to classify capitalization varies read among brokers, advisors, or institutions, but the chart below gives you a typical example of how stocks are defined as small, mid, or large-cap.

Market-Cap	Total Capitalization
Small-Cap	Under $500 million
Mid-Cap	$500 million to 3 billion
Large-Cap	More than 3 billion

Stocks from the three classifications typically vary in degrees of volatility and growth potential. Large-cap stocks are issued by big, established companies with less room for growth. Altogether, the stocks from large cap companies total more than one-half the value of all U.S. stocks. Large cap stocks include well known names such as General Electric, IBM, Wal-Mart, Pfizer, and Microsoft.

Mid-cap stocks offer more room for growth than larger cap stocks but with more stability than a small-cap. Mid-cap stocks include names like Hilton Hotels, Verisign, Staples, and Diebold. They also include lesser known regional companies and banks.

Small-cap stocks are usually more volatile. Most Initial Public Offerings are for small-cap companies. Small-caps offer the potential for significant losses or gains.

International Stocks

You will want to include some international stock in your portfolio. The purchase of stocks in companies that are not tied closely to the U.S. economy additional diversification to your portfolio.

Bonds

Bonds are promissory notes issued by three types of entities: corporations, U.S. government, and state and local government. Returns from government and corporate bonds are taxable, but income earned from most municipal bonds

(bonds used to fund public projects like sewers, bridges, roads, and schools) is tax-free under the Internal Revenue Code. Bonds may be stable and could help to balance out your portfolio. Keep in mind that safe does not mean risk-free. You could lose your investment on some bonds if the issuer defaults. Bonds also lose value when interest rates increase. You could further reduce your risks with bond purchases by choosing a mix of bond types. With proper asset allocation, you won't need to worry about losing everything because your portfolio will be balanced to help manage the risks. Another way to manage risk is to diversify by purchasing a bond fund. Bond funds are mutual funds which hold bonds of multiple issues and use large pools of investor money to increase their buying power and diversify their holdings. When choosing a bond fund, be sure you understand what types of bonds the fund purchases. Read the prospectus carefully.

There are four types of bonds: short-term, intermediate-term, long-term, and high-yield. Short-term bonds typically come due, or mature, in less than three years. Money market funds are often short-term bond funds. These funds are highly liquid allowing you quick access to your money. They typically offer extremely low earnings. Short-term bond funds are good vehicles for holding money for a limited time while you determine what to do with it. Intermediate-term bonds usually mature in three to ten years. If interest rates are declining, long-term bonds (bonds that mature in ten years or more) may offer a good alternative to stocks.

The riskiest class of bonds is high-yield, sometimes referred to as "junk" bonds. They're definitely not right for all investors, but owning a small amount of high yield bonds might be good for your portfolio. High yield bonds are usually issued by corporations or municipalities that receive a "speculative" credit rating but also pay a high rate of interest, usually greater than other types of bonds, if they do not default. These issuers are usually smaller companies with a spotty record or limited ability to pay principal and interest. Junk bonds tend to move with the stock market as they are tied closely to the underlying company's stock performance if they are publicly traded issues. You can spread out the risk of high yield bonds by purchasing shares in a high-yield bond mutual fund that invests in several companies.

The allocation of assets that works for you now will not necessarily be right for you later. For example, many residents will begin with an asset allocation that is 80% stocks and 20% bonds, with the stock further distributed -- according to individual goals -- among large-cap value, large-cap growth and small-cap, for example. Older physicians may reallocate their assets to a 60% stock and 40% bond portfolio in order to reduce risk.

Besides determining whether or not your asset allocation plan matches your goals, you will also need to rebalance your portfolio at least once a year to be certain that your assets maintain the correct allocation. If your stocks grow in value, the result drives up the total portion of your assets allocated to stocks, thus knocking your asset allocation out of alignment. During rebalancing, you will sell any assets that are off balance and use the proceeds to buy assets in the other classes as needed to maintain your proper allocation.

Many investors never rebalance their portfolios, leaving them at risk for great loss. Selling a strong performer seems counterintuitive for many investors. Yet, if you set up your portfolio under a 60% - 40% stock and bond allocation, when your stocks perform so well that they make up 80% of your portfolio, you have moved inadvertently to a much more aggressive position.

Investors who understand and want to benefit from rebalancing often simply forget to do so. Many of our clients avoid this problem by setting a yearly check-up appointment with us the same time each year. In this manner, they aren't any more likely to overlook this important financial task than they are a yearly physical, a birthday, or a time change for daylight savings.

You can determine your current portfolio's asset allocation online. Morningstar offers an Instant X-Ray tool at www.morningstar.com that will use input regarding your portfolio to calculate your current asset allocation. You can use the Instant X-ray results to see if your current portfolio might be ready for an allocation tune-up.

Understand How Asset Classes React with Each Other

Financial professionals describe asset classes as showing negative or positive correlation. The type of correlation helps determine the amount of risk involved in the portfolio mix. This determination depends upon identifying two asset classes that either work opposite of each other, or move in the same direction. The way the assets work together determines the aggressiveness or conservativeness of your portfolio. Understanding your correlation is an important part of your investment strategy.

Maintaining the same asset allocation over time is like a patient taking the same medications prescribed as a young adult throughout her life: it's right at one time but possibly inappropriate for the long-term. Asset allocation will change over time as your goals change. Putting your money into the right mix of asset classes will help you maximize the return on your investment while reducing the risk. The right mix for your portfolio is something that you will decide with your financial planner. As a team, you'll decide which mix of assets meets your goals: either managing risk or capitalizing on the market. Your portfolio should be monitored and adjusted to maintain the right mix.

Establish a Relationship with an Investment Advisor

Your patients can get prescription drugs in Mexico, but would you endorse managing an illness by becoming your own doctor? Why would you do the equivalent with your financial health? Don't go it alone. An investment or financial advisor can help you choose the right distribution of your funds into the right investment vehicles and asset classes. Find a qualified individual whom you can trust to help you make the most of your money. Ask other residents and physicians for recommendations. If you can find an advisor who specializes in financial needs of physicians, you'll have someone on board who understands how your profession impacts your financial health. Such an advisor is best suited to helping you meet your goals during residency and throughout your career.

Develop an Exit Strategy

We've heard numerous tales from our clients about a hot investment tip they received from another physician. It's not uncommon for a client to tell us that he made an investment decision based on a tip picked up in a hospital cafeteria, for example. Physicians are often recipients of investment tips because they tend to have funds to invest. Before you embark on any investment, recognize that the most important component of any investment strategy should be to review your goals to create an exit strategy. A surgeon wouldn't begin to cut without knowing how to suture the incision, nor should you buy an investment without an exit strategy in place. Work with your investment advisor to create your plan. Together you should determine your goals for the invested money. What's right for that money today is not necessarily a good investment in the future.

Your goals will need to be considered alongside factors such as market conditions, your risk level, and interest rates. Regardless of what investments you choose, perform your due diligence and consult your professional advisor to develop an exit strategy before you invest. A good deal isn't a good deal until you sell and reap the rewards. An investment tip may sound dazzling, but if you don't devise a plan for selling before you buy, then you leave yourself open for a bad investment and a subsequent loss of investment dollars.

With your advisor's assistance, create a goal that includes an exit strategy. You don't make or lose anything until you sell. Before you buy, have a clearly articulated, written plan for selling the investment.

Chapter Six

Tax Planning

Proper planning for taxes will allow you to maximize your earnings by limiting your tax liability.

Goal

Use investment vehicles and legal structures to control your taxes now and in retirement.

As a physician, your income will result in a large tax burden. Of course, you should never attempt to hide your income, but tax shelters available within legal guidelines can minimize your tax bill and create more opportunities for your money to work for you. Legitimate tax shelters involve an actual investment with some degree of risk. Any tax shelter with a guaranteed return is probably suspect. At some point in your career, as you begin to amass wealth, we guarantee that someone will tell you about a tax shelter that sounds too good to be true. Trust that instinct.

There are many safe, established tax shelters available to you, which you probably underutilize, such as contributing the maximum allowed amount to your retirement accounts. Any legitimate investment vehicle that allows you to reduce your current or future tax liability should be a part of your tax plan.

Tax planning is closely aligned with retirement planning. By understanding which investments and which legal structures offer the best tax shelters, you'll gain control over taxes on your income and assets. (Retirement and estate planning complement tax planning and will be covered in Chapters Eight and Nine.) A professional advisor can help you build a tax plan that utilizes legitimate tax shelters to reduce your taxes through recognized and legal means. Ben Franklin knew that death and taxes were the only things in life that were inevitable, but with good medicine and good tax planning, they can both be postponed.

Tools

Retirement Accounts

Student Loan Interest Deductions

Home Equity Loans

LLC/LLP

FLP

Trusts

Generation Skipping

Charitable Remainder Trusts (CRTs)

Whole and Variable Life Insurance

Strategy

Develop a Relationship with a Professional Advisor

We've made the case throughout this book for working with a

professional advisor. Even if it seems out of reach now, the hardships you're facing during your residency will bring enormous returns in your future. Once you attain the monetary rewards for all these years of work, study, and more work, you don't want to see your income dwindle unnecessarily. Even worse, you don't want to take advice from a colleague or from a seminar geared to selling tax planning kits for physicians that leave you at odds with the IRS. Using the services of a knowledgeable financial advisor will prevent both options from becoming a reality.

Fill Your Buckets

Think of tax control as a process of filling buckets. Your goal is to distribute your income on a regular basis among three buckets: taxable, pre-tax, and tax-free. By filling all of your tax buckets appropriately, you ensure that all three can be tapped for a return in a way that minimizes your tax liability.

Taxable Bucket

You have already paid taxes on the income you pour into this bucket, and when you draw the income from these investments, the gain on the money you take out is taxable. Investments in this bucket could include: CDs, money market accounts, mutual funds, and stocks. These investment tools are all purchased with after-tax dollars; you've already paid taxes on the money used to make these investments.

Pre-Tax Bucket

Fill this bucket with pre-tax dollars used to purchase investments under individual retirement plans and employer sponsored plans including IRAs, SEP IRAs, and 403(b)s, for example. Unlike the investments in the taxable bucket, you purchase these investments with pre-tax dollars. You paid no taxes on the income used to buy the investment, but when you withdraw these funds in retirement, you will pay taxes on the investment at your tax bracket during retirement.

Tax-Free Bucket

In your Tax-Free bucket are life insurance, tax exempt bonds and funds, and Roth IRAs. These products are purchased with after-tax dollars, and all withdrawals could be tax-free in retirement.

The goal of filling your tax buckets is to control your tax bracket in retirement. You can use the tax buckets to help you reduce your taxable income in retirement with a little planning today. Before you retire, you want to pour as much money as possible into your Pre-Tax bucket, which reduces your tax burden now. You'll also want to pour a generous amount into your Tax-Free bucket to reduce your tax liabilities in retirement. Your taxable bucket serves as a holding tank for your liquid investments that you plan to use for your shorter term goals. By keeping all of your buckets full, you'll receive the most from your tax plan.

Know Your Pre-Retirement Tax Control Options

Know and use every legitimate tax control option available to you during your working years. Here are some good options:

Retirement Accounts

Whether or not you can set up a deductible IRA depends upon your income and the retirement plan options available through your employer. If you are eligible, contribute the maximum amount allowed to your deductible IRA, one of the safest and most recognized tax shelters available. Deductible IRAs belong in the pre-tax bucket. Every dollar you deposit into your IRA may translate into significant tax savings for you now. If your employer offers a 401(k), 403B, profit sharing, etc., you should definitely maximize your contributions. Many of these plans have employer matching programs in which your contributions are matched. These plans typically have a vesting schedule which determines how long you must stay with your employer before you can claim the matching funds as your own. If you leave the employer before your matching funds are fully vested, you can rollover your retirement funds but the matching funds will not rollover into your new account. These plans are sometimes called the company's "golden handcuffs" because the vesting schedule encourages employees' longevity.

If you are not taking advantage of such a program, you are walking away from money on the table. If you have a hard time contributing to your retirement account, try to set it up on an automatic withdrawal program. If the money is taken out of your checking account or paycheck automatically, you may never miss the dollars.

Once you have established your retirement account, continue to fund (to the maximum deductible amount) at regular intervals, using the proper asset allocation. Remember to rebalance your account at least once a year. Small changes in the balance of your portfolio could reap big rewards. Making a simple change to your account could also protect you from major losses.

Student Loan Interest Deductions

A little knowledge about tax planning can help you reduce your income taxes even as a resident. For example, you're probably aware that interest paid on student loans is deductible on your income tax. You lose this deduction if your income level rises above a set amount ($41,500 in 2004). Once you are earning more than that amount, it may make sense to defer your student loans, which causes you to lose your interest deduction. If paying off your school loans and keeping a deduction is your top priority, you can consider a home equity loan. Interest on home equity loans is also deductible. Use the loan to pay off your student loan, and you've preserved your deduction for the loans without worrying about the IRS's income limit.

Purchase Whole or Variable Universal Life Insurance

Recall that these life insurance policies invest a portion of your premium in underlying investments. The cash value of these policies accrues tax deferred, and any gains to the policy's cash value (beyond the amount of premiums paid) are tax-free, if managed correctly. Whole life and variable life insurance offer the benefits of insurance plus additional tax control.

Use Family Limited Partnerships (FLP)

The Family Limited Partnership (FLP) is an excellent tool for tax control, asset protection, and estate planning. In an FLP, all family assets are transferred to the partnership, and the husband and/or wife are named general partners in the trust. Other family members are named limited partners. General partners make all decisions regarding trust management and investments. Limited partners have no say in these decisions, so parents don't need to worry about giving control of their assets to their children. The FLP allows you to shelter income in retirement by gifting a percent interest in the partnership to your children. Gifting a minority interest in the business allows you to discount the value of the gift. More than likely, you are not ready to take advantage of the tax benefits of an FLP, but, as your assets grow, this might become an important vehicle for asset protection and estate planning. Learn more about this powerful tax control tool in order to plan for its use later in your career. Make sure to consult your financial advisor, your attorney, and your CPA when setting up an FLP.

Know Your Tax Shelter Options for Retirement

The way you legally structure the ownership of your assets can offer you additional tax control. The creation of corporations and trusts for tax planning is beyond the scope of this book. Each state regulates trusts and corporations differently. Your tax shelter options provide a range of excellent tools that may double as estate planning and asset protection tools. We recommend that you learn more about these options and discuss which vehicles afford you the greatest tax relief.

> Limited Liability Partnership
> Family Limited Partnership
> Trusts:
>> Irrevocable
>> Revocable
>> Generation Skipping
>> Charitable Trusts

After residency, your income will accelerate right along with your tax bill. Proper tax planning now will allow you to enjoy and accumulate more of your earnings.

Chapter Seven

Retirement

It's never too early to plan for retirement. Careful planning now can allow you to maintain the lifestyle you desire in retirement.

Goal

Create a portfolio of retirement accounts that will deliver the maximum wealth accumulation and the desired amount of retirement income when you're ready to hang up your stethoscope.

It's difficult to think seriously about the end of your career when you're just beginning. Especially now, when you don't have much extra cash, it's easy to postpone retirement planning.

Do not do it. The sooner you begin planning for your retirement, the larger your assets will be when you finally call it quits. Consider the following: If you start investing $100 a month at age 25 and continue to invest this amount until age 65, with an 8% interest rate, you will have $335,751. If you wait only five years and begin the same tax-deferred investment plan at age 30, your investment grows to only $223, 332. The extra five years of investing requires only an additional $6,000 of your funds but increases the account's total value by more than $100,000. Time is a powerful investment tool.

Most individuals postpone retirement planning because it seems unimportant. Others understand the exponential power of compounding interest and reinvested income dividends but simply don't get around to starting their retirement investing. If you've met your cash reserve and purchased adequate disability and life insurance, you're well on your way to helping create and preserve your wealth. If you've got a little left over, maintain your current savings deduction, but direct it toward your retirement planning. Remember that investing in your retirement may also reduce your tax bill, so you can approach your retirement contributions as a way to increase your net earnings.

Tools

Roth IRA

401(k), 403(b), 457

IRA

SEP-IRA

SIMPLE Plan

Universal Life Insurance

Municipal Bonds

Annuities

Moonlighting

Strategy

Review the Tax Buckets

You'll recall that the goal with tax planning, as represented by our tax buckets, is to reduce your tax burden. By investing in vehicles that yield tax-free benefits, you can reduce your tax bill in retirement. The vehicles purchased with after-tax dollars that provide tax free yields at retirement are: life insurance; tax exempt bonds; and Roth IRAs.

Start Now

Start your retirement plan as early in your career as possible. Today isn't too soon. The most important factors in your retirement plan are the level of risk you choose to take and the time you give your investment to grow. The sooner you start investing, the more your money grows. Yes, it may seem impossible to consider putting money away for retirement when you've got so much student loan debt and money's already tight, but starting now will make an enormous difference later. We've already shown you one example of the power of compounding interest.

A Tale of Two Doctors

At 25, Dr. Perez's cash was in short demand. Nonetheless, she knew she wanted to begin investing for her retirement immediately. She opened an IRA at her local credit union and deposited $2,000 every year for ten years. At that time she became pregnant with her first child and took a break from her investment strategy to use some of her investing funds to prepare for the arrival of her baby.

Dr. Perez's colleague, Dr. Riccard, had been studying personal finance and knew that at age 35 he was getting an early start on his retirement investments. He opened an IRA and began to contribute $2,000 each year until age 65. He often boasted to Dr. Perez that his early start would allow him to gain much more than her.

At age 65, they were both surprised to learn that, even though Dr. Perez never made another additional deposit into her account, and even though she contributed $42,000 less than her colleague, her account's value at retirement was $376,956 compared to Dr. Riccard's $282,975. Dr. Perez's only regret was that she had not continued her early investing momentum.

Create Your Plan

You already know from Chapter Five how important it is to start with an exit strategy when investing. Retirement planning demands the same. Set your goals for retirement and then draft the plan that will take you there.

Many people advise that you will need less income in retirement than your pre-retirement income, anywhere from 70% to 90%. It's our experience that this assumption does not always hold up. True, you'll no longer need to pay for life insurance or a mortgage, more than likely, but your health care costs may rise in retirement, and you'll have a lifestyle that you'll probably want to maintain. How do you expect to fill all those extra hours? You'll probably need money to pay for your expanded leisure opportunities.

You can use internet tools to help you determine your retirement needs. Many financial websites offer retirement calculators that do this for you including www.reimanfinancial.com, www.money.com, and www.401k.com. Your financial advisor can also work with you to create a retirement plan. Your advisor will help you calculate how much money you'll be able to retire with based on your current income, investments, and savings levels. You'll also want to consider other needs that may arise, impacting your ability to save for retirement, such as planning for a child's educational needs and caring for aging parents. You can also factor in any benefits from Social Security. The current structure of the Social Security program will need to change to maintain its solvency in the future. How these changes impact future benefits is unknown. Younger physicians should consider Social Security benefits as icing on the retirement cake since the program will more than likely change significantly in the next decades. Once you determine how much retirement you can afford (this amount will invariably change), you can compare this to the amount of retirement income you desire. You may need to make adjustments to bring these two figures in line. This calculation should not be taken lightly. Spend ample time calculating your needs in retirement. If you build your retirement plan around a number that has not been calculated thoughtfully, you may arrive at retirement to find that you don't have enough money available to meet your needs.

Fund a Roth IRA

Traditional deductible Individual Retirement Accounts (IRAs) belong in the pre-tax bucket. You use pre-tax dollars to contribute, and the money grows tax-deferred until you withdraw it at retirement. Roth IRAs belong in the tax-free bucket as they are purchased with after-tax dollars and are withdrawn tax-free. (You can access any principal contributed to a contributory Roth IRA without incurring penalties since the contributions came from after-tax dollars. Interest earned on the principal does have penalties if withdrawn early.) You will definitely want to take advantage of the opportunity to earn tax-free income, but you have to start right now. As a physician, you only have a tiny window for this potent tax saving opportunity.

In 2006, you may only contribute to a Roth IRA if your Adjusted Gross Income (AGI) is less than $110,000, if you are single, and $160,000 if you are married filing jointly. The amount you are allowed to contribute decreases once your adjusted gross income exceeds $95,000 if you are single and $150,000 for joint filers. (You can find your current contribution limits by requesting Publication 590 from the Internal Revenue Service at www.irs. gov.) In 2006, if you are eligible for a Roth, you may contribute up to $4,000 annually, if you are single, or up to $8,000 if you are married filing jointly. The IRS also allows persons over 50 to make additional catch-up contributions.

If you already have an IRA, you may want to consider converting it to a Conversion Roth IRA. You'll be required to pay ordinary income taxes on the amount converted, but the tax-free benefits may outweigh the tax burden today. To determine if this option is advantageous to your situation, ask your financial planner or use the IRA conversion calculator available at www.reimanfinancial.com. In 2006, the Adjusted Gross Income limit to convert a Roth IRA is $100,000 for singles or married individuals filing jointly. Paying a little extra on your current tax bill may generate big rewards in retirement, so definitely explore the option if you have an IRA.

Once you complete your residency and your income increases dramatically, your Roth window of opportunity slams shut. Talk with your financial planner now about funding a Roth IRA so that you don't miss out on the powerful tax-free benefits offered by this tool. If you max out your Roth contributions while you're eligible, those contributions should have compounding, tax-deferred growth and reinvested dividends, and will deliver tax free money at retirement.

Max-out Your 401(k), 403(b), or 457 Plan

If you have a 401(k), or 403(b), or 457 plan, take advantage of it. These are all types of employer-sponsored retirement savings plans. 403(b)s may be offered by non-profit organizations. 457s may be offered by government organizations and 401(k)s may be offered by other types of employers. Some of these plans offer employer matching contributions. Employers in these plans contribute a certain percent to match the employee's contributions. If you are eligible for one of these plans, try to at least contribute to the matching amount. Your money grows tax-deferred in these accounts and is fully taxable when it is withdrawn. If your employer matches contributions, then you are getting the equivalent of free money. Of course, you must be vested to take advantage of your employer's contributions. Your vesting schedule will outline how long it takes for you to become vested in your accounts. After that time, the money is yours and can be rolled over into a new Rollowver IRA when you leave your employer. If you leave the employer prior to becoming 100% vested, the employer's portion is not available to you for a roll-over account. These accounts are powerful retirement tools that most people underutilize.

Some small employers offer a Savings Incentive Match Plan for Employees (SIMPLE). SIMPLE plans also offer varying amounts of employer matching contributions. Take advantage of the plan and contribute the maximum amount allowed.

Create A Simplified Employee Pension (SEP) Plan

If you are self-employed, you can take advantage of the power of a SEP IRA. Self-employed individuals create SEP plans for themselves and their employees. SEP plans are similar to traditional IRAs but offer much higher contribution limits. Under current contribution limits, self-employed individuals may contribute up to $41,000 into a SEP IRA. SEP IRAs may be the most advantageous way to put away significant pre-tax dollars for retirement. Check with your financial or tax advisor to determine if you can take advantage of these powerful tools.

Open a Roth IRA

Invest enough to receive matching contributions from your employer-provided retirement plan, and then consider funding a Roth IRA while you still can. For information about investment vehicles for your IRAs visit www.morningstar.com or speak with your investment advisor.

Start Saving Now, Automatically

Make a pledge to your future. Take a portion of every check and put it into your retirement savings. If you haven't already started an automatic savings plan, start one now. People tend to live to the full extent of their means. A person who lives on $20,000 one year will not save an extra $10,000 if his income jumps to $30,000 the next year. He adjusts his spending to match his income. You will adjust your spending to match the reduced income that results from your automatic savings. By engaging in forced savings now, you'll establish the habit for future years and will never miss the extra discretionary income. It'll be quietly tucked away growing into a healthy nest egg. Sign-up for automatic withdrawals from your paycheck, if this option is available to you, or arrange to have monthly contributions drafted electronically from your bank account.

Explore Annuities and Municipal Bonds

Let's return for a moment to the tax buckets. We filled the taxable bucket with vehicles purchased with after-tax dollars and taxed at withdrawal. These options could include: CDs, mutual funds, bank savings accounts, and money market accounts. You probably have, or will have, your cash reserve in one of these accounts. However, these options aren't very beneficial for retirement planning as they offer little tax relief.

We also included annuities in this bucket. An annuity is a contract between you and your insurance carrier that offers you either a fixed or variable rate of return. The annuity benefit will either grow (accumulation) or you can annuitize. An accumulated annuity works like a mutual fund: the money is invested and increases or decreases based on the underlying investment vehicle's performance. An annuitized benefit pays out a series of pre-arranged payments based on the contract with the insurance company. People often misunderstand annuities because of their complex nature. The important thing to note about an annuity is that it is a contract with a life insurance company; it costs more than some other investment vehicles but could offer additional benefits that other products may not. Annuities can be expensive but may meet your needs. Annuity buyers can purchase special features to add-on to their policies, and some policies offer guaranteed rates. Annuities also offer asset protection; some states shield annuities from creditors. You should discuss annuities with your advisor to determine if they can help you meet your needs.

Insurance companies offer annuities as a way to accumulate or distribute wealth for retirement. The decision to invest in annuities is one which a financial advisor can best help you evaluate.

Municipal bonds (discussed in Chapter Five), also called "debt securities", are simply loans made to the insurer by an investor. They are promissory notes between a government entity and an investor in which the government entity promises to repay the borrowed amount plus interest. The amount of interest is determined at the time the bond is issued. The entity agrees to pay at "maturity"-- a specified period in time. Bonds can be an excellent addition to your retirement portfolio. They could provide a source of income with a rate generally higher than other short-term investments. Municipal bonds can offer federal tax-free returns in retirement.

Find More Money to Contribute

If you have a difficult time finding money to contribute to your retirement, don't overlook some easy options like the following short list.

Free-up extra income by paying off credit card debt or consolidating student loans.

If you're spending is not controlled, go back to your budget (Chapter One).

Increase your retirement savings by increasing your income. Income made from moonlighting can be earmarked for additional retirement money.

Income earned by a spouse or by other family members can also be used to increase retirement savings.

Contribute all gifts received to your retirement account.

If you pay off a loan, such as your car, keep making the payment by depositing the same amount into your retirement account. You're already in the habit of parting with the amount, so it'll be painless.

Cut back on one expense item and put all the money saved into your retirement account. For example, make coffee at home and put the three dollars a day you save from not buying lattes at a coffee shop into an envelope. At the end of the month, contribute the entire amount to your retirement fund.

Don't Touch It

Typically, tax benefit accounts have stiff early withdrawal penalties that you should never encounter because your cash reserve should be adequate. In addition, you should be properly covered by disability and life insurance. Yet, in case of a cash crunch, don't fall back on your retirement funds. Consider them sacred. Put money into your tax deferred accounts and leave it there. If you leave a position with a company that provided a 401(k), 403 (b), 457, or SIMPLE Plan, consider rolling it over into an IRA. This allows you to control the investment and frees it from the plan document restrictions. Don't touch those funds until it's time to withdraw them in retirement.

Evaluate your Plan and Adjust

Reevaluate your retirement goals and progress once a year. As your financial circumstances change, so will your plan. A long-term relationship with a financial advisor will help you maintain a long-range retirement plan. As with other investment accounts, you'll need to rebalance your portfolio regularly. Work with your advisor to determine if and when you need to change your asset allocation.

Missteps

Waiting to start your retirement investing is perhaps the biggest mistake you can make. Consider the compounding interest stories in this chapter, and start investing for your retirement now.

When planning for retirement, you'll need to be sure you don't outlive your money. Retirees are living longer and longer.

Chapter Eight

Asset Protection

Protecting your assets from judgment (related to malpractice and/or non-medical circumstances), transferring ownership, and making yourself a less desirable target for lawsuits help you preserve and maintain your wealth.

Goal

Properly protect assets and avoid being a target for litigation using asset protection strategies.

The unfortunate reality for you as a physician is that, at some point in your career, you are likely to become the target of a lawsuit. Tort reform might impact malpractice rates, but the extent of this impact won't be known for many years. Malpractice suits are not the only threat. Your assets could be reduced as a result of a failed marriage, a bad investment or partnership, or inadvertent participation in a tax scheme. The perception of physicians as defendants with deep pockets makes you a more attractive proposition for an attorney deciding to take a case on contingency. If the attorney sees an opportunity to seize assets you own, he might agree to take the case. Even if you're not in a high litigation specialty, your assets are at risk, and not only from malpractice claims. An ugly divorce or a bad investment deal may stand a chance of dissolving your wealth.

Judgments on family matters, civil actions or liability from injuries on your real estate could erode your vulnerable assets. So, rather than wait and wonder when you might be targeted, you can be pro-active, building and implementing an asset protection plan that insulates you from judgments as much as possible. By insulating yourself from risk and shielding your assets from creditors, you establish a level of protection that allows you to practice medicine confidently. Proper asset protection planning will also enable you to explore attractive investment and business opportunities without risking loss of accumulated wealth.

Please note that this chapter addresses general concepts relating to asset protection and does not offer legal advice. The laws that govern the extent to which a strategy protects an asset vary from state to state. You should consult an attorney before executing any asset protection strategy to insure that you accomplish your goals.

Tools

Malpractice Insurance
Umbrella Insurance
Trusts
Limited Liability Companies (LLC)/Professional
Corporations (PC)/Limited Partnerships (LP)
Family Limited Partnerships (FLP)
Properly Titled Assets
Homestead Exemptions
Annuities and Life Insurance
Gifting
Accounts Receivable (A/R) Protection

Strategy

Build Rapport with Patients to Help Avoid Lawsuits

Every new patient represents an opportunity for a malpractice lawsuit. You have probably already seen and heard enough to believe that a malpractice suit is inevitable at some point in your career. Malpractice litigation continues to rise. Despite tort reform, plaintiffs' attorneys are still increasingly willing to accept malpractice cases as medicine becomes more complex. These factors, combined with the impersonal nature of the patient and physician relationship, may be contributing to the trend in malpractice litigation, but there are steps you can take that will limit the likelihood of a malpractice suit.

Patients rarely sue doctors they like. Studies of malpractice suits against physicians have demonstrated a link between physicians with many patient complaints and a high occurrence of malpractice suits. (See "Patient Complaints and Malpractice Risk" in JAMA, June 12, 2002.) The fact is that doctors with better interpersonal skills are sued less often. Doctors who build rapport with their patients and treat them with respect, empathy, and honesty are less likely to be malpractice targets.

Making patient satisfaction a top priority in your practice will help prevent most malpractice claims before they are initiated. If a patient does leave your office upset, your office manager can follow up to determine what the problem is and how to rectify the situation. This system may prevent small issues from turning into expensive and detrimental lawsuits.

You can also mange your risks by knowing your patients. You may not want to take on aggressive or demanding patients. If you choose to accept patients of this type, you should always deal with them as potential litigants, recognizing the risks from the outset of treatment. You can also obtain litigation searches for a small fee from companies that provide this service. These searches indicate whether any potential patients have sued other physicians, representing a potential threat to you.

Many malpractice suits are introduced after a physician fails to deliver on her promise of favorable results, so never guarantee results. If the promise is not realized, your patient will believe that the lack of results was related to your malpractice, and a lawsuit may follow.

Always maintain impeccable records. Thorough and complete records are your best defense against malpractice claims, offering explanation for less than favorable outcomes. When dealing with a patient whose results were not positive, use caution when discussing the situation with the patient. An admission can be used as evidence against you in court and may encourage the patient to file a lawsuit that otherwise might have been avoided. Preventing malpractice claims by building rapport and interpersonal skills may be one of the smartest and most cost-effective asset protection strategies available to you.

Purchase Adequate Insurance

Adequate insurance is the foundation for any solid asset protection plan. You should purchase and maintain adequate automobile and homeowner's insurance policies. A general liability policy will protect against injury claims made by visitors to your property such as a patient slipping and falling on a wet floor.

Malpractice insurance is an essential asset protection tool. Juries have awarded plaintiffs large judgments against attending physicians for the actions of first-year residents. Consult with your financial planner to determine the right amount of insurance for your specialty. Malpractice insurance differs from other types of insurance. When choosing a malpractice policy, check the following features:

Scope: Covered acts are defined by your policy. Most policies cover all acts of professional negligence but may exclude liabilities arising from acts of assault and battery, defamation, invasion of privacy, and illegal activity. Be sure you know your policy's scope of coverage.

Term: The term varies on different policies. Some policies cover claims when the liability occurs regardless of the date the lawsuit is filed ("occurrence-made"). "Claims made" policies cover claims filed during the policy year despite the date the malpractice occurs. Most private policies are claims-made. Understand the term of your policy to prevent gaps in coverage for previous acts of malpractice that may occur if you switch policies or retire. If you leave a position under which you had a claims-made policy, you'll need to purchase "tail" coverage, which protects you from any claims made after you terminate the current coverage. We'll discuss tail coverage in more detail in Chapter 10.

Deductibles: The deductible is the portion paid by the physician before the insurance begins to pay. The deductible amount varies greatly from one policy to the next. Most physicians choose policies that offer larger deductibles with reduced premiums. This option allows physicians to maintain a higher level of coverage.

Like other physicians, you may consider employment with HMOs or institutional employers to take advantage of free malpractice insurance. Is an employer-provided malpractice policy enough to protect you? Unfortunately, not always. The employer's carrier may not be required to defend or pay judgments against employees. Before going this route, be certain to read the employer's policy to determine that the policy obligates the insurance company to defend you against claims. Also check that the level of coverage can withstand a large judgment, bearing in mind that astronomical jury awards of more than $1 million are becoming more frequent. If the employer's policy can't hold up to a one million dollar judgment, supplement the coverage with an additional individual policy. You may also want to evaluate the financial strength of the employer. Organizations with financial problems may be forced to lower their coverage or cancel policies, leaving you vulnerable to malpractice claims.

Even physicians who feel they're adequately insured against malpractice claims may find that their claims are denied because they either fall outside the policy's scope of coverage or because the claim is not reported according to the policy's guidelines. So understand your policy before you purchase.

To counter the exploding costs of malpractice premiums, some physicians are choosing to forgo malpractice insurance and are "going bare". Premiums for some specialties can cost more than $100,000 annually. Even a policy that costs a fraction of that can be cost prohibitive for many physicians. To avoid enormous premiums, some physicians gamble and go without, betting that they will not get sued. You should pursue this option only if your assets are completely protected and you have the ability to pay the costs of defending a lawsuit. (Bear in mind that even a frivolous lawsuit could cost you up to $100,000 in legal fees.)

Some physicians decide to go bare as a deterrent to lawsuits. One might argue that this choice seems to work. Statistics prove that malpractice insurance encourages lawsuits. When faced with a lawsuit, you will be asked to report the amount of your malpractice policy in the first phase of the litigation. Many attorneys will be less likely to pursue a case if a large settlement does not appear possible. The statistics indicate that, in cases against uninsured physicians, patients usually settle for less.

We believe that going bare should be a last resort. Before going bare, you may be able to make changes to your policy that allow you to lower your premiums and/or raise your deductibles keeping coverage intact. If you are over-insured, lower your coverage limits.

Relocating your practice to a nearby county may also help reduce the cost of your malpractice premiums.

If you decide to practice without malpractice coverage, you will need to determine how the decision to go bare will affect your practice. You'll probably be forced to convert to a cash practice, and you will more than likely lose your hospital privileges. Many people are unfamiliar with umbrella coverage, an essential asset protection tool available at a modest premium. Umbrella coverage will cover claims that exceed the policy limits on other standard policies like homeowners and automobile insurance. Another advantage to umbrella coverage is that an attorney may pursue the limits of the umbrella policy leaving your assets intact. Discuss umbrella coverage with your insurance agent.

Act Early and Get Professional Advice

We cannot emphasize enough the importance of planning now for any future litigation. If you initiate asset protection strategies after a lawsuit has been threatened or a judgment appears imminent, you may be guilty of "fraudulent conveyance". Simply transferring the family residence's title to your spouse's name after a litigation threat is revealed can place your assets at risk under "fraudulent conveyance".

You have chosen a profession that will place you at risk for litigation. Plan now for the possibility using expert advice. Follow the letter of the law when making any asset protection decisions. You may receive information regarding seminars or kits marketed specifically for the asset protection needs of physicians. Proceed with caution. Seek input from your attorney, financial planner, and tax accountant to avoid illegal schemes or asset protection strategies that could cost you greatly and still leave you vulnerable. We'll review some of the strategies that are typically well-suited to physicians, but you should discuss any of these strategies with your professional advisors and begin all asset protection plans when you are judgment-free.

Dr. Tyson Protects Her Assets too Late in the Game

Dr. McBride attended an asset protection seminar for physicians at a local association meeting. He recognized that his assets were vulnerable and immediately worked with an attorney and a financial advisor to initiate a solid asset protection plan. It had not been cheap, but he felt that he could practice with greater confidence knowing that his assets wouldn't be wiped out in a lawsuit. Dr. Tyson had heard about Dr. McBride's asset protection plan and believed that it was just another way for people to prey on doctors with deep pockets. She had felt that "asset protection" was the trend of the day and was too expensive and too much of a hassle to be worthwhile. One day during surgery, Dr. Tyson appeared distraught, and Dr. McBride asked her what was wrong. Dr. Tyson informed him that she was being sued by a former patient, and she was worried that she might lose everything. Dr. McBride confided that her fear was the reason he moved early to initiate an asset protection plan. He encouraged Dr. Tyson to start one of her own. Desperate and worried, Dr. Tyson made an appointment with an attorney and a financial advisor and initiated an aggressive asset protection plan. This decision turned out to be unwise: she was soon investigated by the IRS. Not only did she lose her lawsuit, but she now faced prosecution for fraudulent conveyance.

Max-Out Your Retirement Accounts

In case we didn't emphasize enough the benefits of maxing-out contributions to your retirement account, here's one more: most pensions and retirement plans are protected from creditors. Qualified plans such as pensions, 401(k), profit sharing and money purchase plans are federally protected. IRAs and life insurance contracts are also protected in several states. Contributing the maximum amount allowed keeps your hard-earned money safe from creditors. This is one more reason to start retirement investing now.

Purchase Annuities and Life Insurance (Some States)

We've already discussed these options as ways to provide for your loved ones. These investment tools also offer additional asset protection in some states. If the policy's cash surrender value or the annuities contract lists your spouse or children as beneficiaries, then the benefits are (usually) sufficiently protected from creditors.

Title Property Correctly

Your creditors can't get assets you don't own. Title your assets so that they'll be beyond creditors' reach. If your state has a generous homestead exemption, then your family residence is sheltered from judgments and creditors. Be sure to review your state's homestead laws carefully. We've known physicians with homes on acreage in unincorporated areas that later were incorporated into municipalities. The result was a change in the homestead exemption levels, leaving the acreage at risk. In some states you can also title your property "tenancy-by-the-entirety". Under tenancy-by-the-entirety, assets owned by both spouses cannot be taken by creditors to satisfy one spouse's obligation. Tenancy–by-the-entirety does have tax consequences and should be reviewed by your professional advisors.

If it is not cost-prohibitive, we also recommend that physicians maintain a home equity line of credit on the residence, making it possible to quickly remove equity from the house if needed. Many physicians ask about placing the home's title in the name of the spouse in cases where the spouse is less vulnerable to liability. We generally don't recommend this strategy because it can create a negative tax consequence and could leave you vulnerable in case of divorce. Courts usually divide joint property equally, but there have been cases where a spouse with title to property has been awarded a greater share of the joint property.

Automobiles and other vehicles are often investigated by creditors early in their search for assets. Title them for maximum protection. We typically suggest that vehicles be titled in the less vulnerable spouse's name or under a separate entity, such as a Family Limited Partnership or a Limited Liability Company, which we'll discuss shortly. If you need to drain equity from a vehicle, this is easily done by refinancing.

Boats, airplanes, and other recreational vehicles are safest if they are co-owned. If you own an airplane with two friends, a creditor is unlikely to want a one-third share of it. Not many people are interested in co-owning a vehicle with total strangers, making it unattractive to the creditor. Large loans on vehicles also make them undesirable because creditors are unlikely to get more than the loan balance for the vehicle.

Gift Your Assets

Gifting is a basic asset protection strategy that you'll want to explore with your advisors. In 2004 individuals could gift $11,000 a year to family members, removing the funds from a creditor's reach. Gifting also reduces estate taxes. (See www.irs.gov for current gifting limits.)

Transfer Your Assets to a Family Limited Partnership

The FLP is an excellent way to shield your bank account, family residence, and other personal and business assets. A FLP works like a business. You transfer ownership of all family assets to the FLP. You and your spouse become controlling partners of the partnership. Other family members can receive limited partnerships. If a judgment is incurred against a partner, all assets in the FLP are safe from seizure, sale, or transfer. To satisfy the judgment, the creditor can ask the courts for a charging order. A charging order requires that any distributions from the partnership be directed to the creditor until the judgment is completely paid. If the FLP is set up for asset protection purposes, the language of the partnership agreement allows partners to withhold distributions at any time. Creditors who request a charging order must also pay federal income tax on phantom income generated by the assets in the partnership. Since most creditors are unlikely to want to incur a tax liability while waiting to receive distributions, many will not request a charging order. FLPs are excellent vehicles for transferring ownership of assets to children without giving up control of those assets. As always, you should consult your financial and legal advisors to see if this type of partnership is right for you.

Use Business Entities to Shelter Assets

You should consider transferring ownership of your assets to different business entities. This doesn't mean you give up control of your assets. It just puts hurdles in front of your assets. You may want to run your practice as a Professional Corporation (PC), which can offer protection from liability for issues other than medical malpractice; a Limited Liability Company (LLC) in which you may not be liable for your partners' actions; or a Limited Partnership (LP), which can also limit your liability. An LLC protects the underlying asset in case a creditor attempts to control it.

By layering entities you are attempting to shield your assets from judgment because the assets are owned by a different entity.

At some point in your career, you're bound to receive an investment tip or business idea that appeals to you. If you decide to pursue it, create an LLC to limit your liability to the amount of your investment. You don't want your financial downfall to be a hot business idea gone sour.

Create Trusts

Trusts can be rather expensive to set up and maintain. Work with your advisors to do a cost-benefits analysis. If the costs do outweigh the benefits, you should consider an alternative strategy such as annuities. If you decide to pursue a trust, you have two types to consider, revocable and irrevocable, each of which creates different income and estate tax consequences. Again your advisors should help you determine if this vehicle is right for you.

There are legal and tax implications to any structure you choose, and these vary from state to state. Consult an attorney before setting up the corporate structure of your practice.

Protect Your Accounts Receivable

Perhaps your most vulnerable asset is your Accounts Receivable. Most physicians are likely to have more than $1 million in accounts receivable at any one time. In the case of a judgment, creditors can reach this valuable asset. Your attorney and financial advisor can help you initiate a plan to help protect this naked asset. Any accounts receivable protection strategies should be undertaken with your advisor's assistance as the IRS is scrutinizing accounts receivable protection more heavily. An attorney and a financial advisor with significant experience with physicians will be able to outline legitimate options for protecting your accounts receivable.

Tip

Set your asset protection plan in place early in your career. You'll be able to accumulate wealth and reduce your fears of losing your wealth. You'll also avoid "fraudulent conveyance" charges by setting up asset protection strategies long before you need the shelters. Seek professional advice and follow the law. With adequate planning, your assets will grow safely, out of reach from creditors or judgments.

Chapter Nine

Estate Planning

Make certain your estate reaches your heirs expeditiously while incurring minimal taxes.

Goal

Use estate planning tools and documents to expedite the transfer of your estate upon your death.

Estate planning aligns with many other financial goals, especially tax and asset protection planning. In order to best plan your estate, you should understand the documents and concepts related to estate planning, as well as what happens to your estate when you die.

Probate is a legal procedure that insures the instructions of your will are carried out. If you die without a will, the courts have the right to decide how to divide your estate and to appoint guardians for your children. These decisions are made in probate. Probate can be costly and time-consuming. Use the recommended strategies to preserve the wealth in your estate and to ensure it passes to your heirs as you desire.

Please note that this chapter addresses general concepts relating to asset protection and does not offer legal advice. The laws that govern the extent to which a strategy protects an asset vary from state to state. You should consult an attorney before executing any asset protection strategy to insure that you accomplish your goals.

Tools

Will

Power of Attorney

Medical Power of Attorney

Financial Inventory

Professional Advisors

Strategy

Build a Team

Estate planning involves the work of a team including an attorney, financial advisor, retirement plan administrator, accountant or tax advisor, and a trust officer. Ask colleagues for references. Once you've assembled your team, be sure that they work in a coordinated effort so that your estate plan works in its entirety.

Prepare Estate Planning Documents and Keep Them Current

You need the following documents to protect your estate:

Will

You should maintain a current will at all times. Update your will at least every five years, or after any significant change in your life. Because probate records are open to public scrutiny, assets listed in your will are vulnerable. Creditors and the IRS can examine your will to find assets. They can also view any documents used in planning your estate unless they are considered privileged communications with your attorney. Do not leave specific dollar amounts to your heirs in your will. Instead express your wishes by indicating a percentage to be given to each heir.

Power of Attorney

This document assigns someone else the ability to make financial and legal decisions on your behalf. This is an extremely powerful document. Be certain to use very specific language to avoid abuse of this power by the designee.

Medical Power of Attorney

This document designates another person to make medical decisions for you in case you become incapacitated. It is often accompanied by a living will, which states your specific requests regarding medical treatment.

Financial Inventory

Create a list of your professional advisors. Include phone numbers and addresses. List insurance policies and investment accounts. Include the location of account documents, the location and number of accounts, and the location of your safety deposit box and key.

Avoid Probate

Not only is probate a costly and time consuming process, but it is also open to public scrutiny. All assets that are held in your name go to probate. Assets with joint tenancy or right of survivorship pass directly to your spouse, another reason to title property correctly. Assets with a designated beneficiary on a contract, such as life insurance, annuities, and retirement funds, pass directly to the beneficiary, usually avoiding probate.

You can avoid probate on the rest of your estate with a revocable or "living" trust mentioned in the previous chapter. A living trust allows you to maintain control over the assets in the trust by acting as trustee. You also have the right to revoke or amend the trust. The living trust (sometimes called a "will substitute") can work in concert with your will. Your will can direct all assets titled in your name to your trust upon your death. From the trust, your heirs access your accumulated wealth exactly as you intended. Another benefit of the living trust is it can ensure that your estate is properly managed if you are incapacitated.

Shelter Your Estate from Taxes

Many of the vehicles we've already discussed can be used to reduce your estate's tax liability. One excellent estate tax planning vehicle that we have not yet mentioned is the Irrevocable Life Insurance Trust (ILIT). An ILIT is an irrevocable trust that, if set up correctly, holds a life insurance policy and allows the insurance proceeds to pass on to your children in a favorable, taxable situation at the time of your death. It should be carefully considered because, as the name suggests, an irrevocable trust cannot be changed. An irrevocable trust requires you to relinquish direct control over the assets you decide to place in the trust.

Discuss with your professional advisors how you can use ILITs and the following vehicles to minimize your estate tax and pass wealth to your heirs:

Gifting

Life Insurance

Annuities

Trusts

Retirement Funds

FLPs

LLCs/LPs

Even though your estate may currently be comprised of more liabilities than assets, planning for the time when your assets exceed your liabilities will allow you to share your accumulated wealth with your loved ones.

Chapter Ten

Negotiating Your Contract

Once you complete your residency, you may be ready to sign the first contract you're offered. Don't take the first offer, and don't sign anything until you've reviewed your contract with a professional advisor and negotiated the best possible deal.

Goal

With the assistance of a contract advisor, use your understanding of contract terms to negotiate an employment agreement that best serves your needs.

Medicine is business. Like most business transactions, the basis of a good medical agreement is a solid and well-negotiated contract. Even the most straightforward employment agreement should be conveyed in a written contract.

A contract is a legally binding, written agreement that clearly identifies the relationship of the parties involved for liability, financial, and other purposes. It is a perfect opportunity to spell out every detail and provision of your work relationship. Although some of the provisions may never be utilized, you want to understand all of them and how they impact your relationship with your employer. Poorly negotiated contracts could cost you thousands or even millions of dollars in earnings over the course of your career. You have an excellent opportunity to negotiate compensation and issues such as partnership, moonlighting, or termination before you establish your relationship and while both parties are happy. By considering the worst possible outcomes before you ever sign a contract, you'll minimize unpleasant surprises during your employment term.

Every contract is drafted to meet the unique needs of the parties involved. Although we're providing you with some general guidelines for contract negotiation, you should hire an attorney and a financial advisor to assist you in this process. This professional advice will help you identify which issues are paramount to your specialty and your personal situation while preventing you from agreeing to terms that may limit or damage your career.

Tools

Contract

Professional Contract Advisor

Strategy

Understand the Terms of a Contract

As you begin your career in medicine, you probably aren't anticipating any problems with your employer. However, if something does go wrong, approaching your employer at that point for clarification about your relationship or employment agreement is probably not going to yield positive results for you or the employer. A written contract spells out the nature of your relationship with the employer and key provisions describing your relationship. A written contract also removes ambiguities from the relationship and identifies what both parties can expect. Identifying all key provisions of your employment up front helps you decide if the employer you're considering shares your goals. If it is critical for you to join a practice that will let you buy-into the partnership, and the proposed contract doesn't mention buying in, you know that you need further written clarification, or possibly you will need to seek a different employment opportunity.

All contracts are negotiable, and your goal is to arrive at an agreement that is fair to you and the employer. Don't take the terms that are first presented to you. In order to negotiate the best possible arrangement, you'll need a clear understanding of the terms commonly included in a physician's contract. If you sign a contract and later realize that it includes provisions that you don't like, you've missed your opportunity to negotiate. Put ample time and money into a thorough review, and you'll start your career with peace of mind knowing that you're on a solid contractual foundation. Here are the terms you are most likely to encounter in a physician's contract:

Start Date: We recommend that our clients choose a start date that is two to three weeks later than your ideal start date. Although you may be anxious to join the employer and start earning money, having a two or three week cushion of time allows you to rest before starting your new position and provides a window for processing of your licensing paperwork. You don't want to miss an employment opportunity because you've given yourself a tight start date and your licensing isn't complete.

Duration: Most contracts cover a one to three year period. We typically advise our clients to negotiate for two year terms for more security. If a practice has financial problems after the first year, under a two-year term your salary will be safe. Under a one-year contract in the same scenario, you may be offered a lower salary in response to the financial troubles of your employer. If your contract is for more than one year and automatically rolls over into the next year, you should amend the provision to cover all contract terms except compensation. You don't want to be locked into your first year's compensation rate for three years. Your compensation should keep up with inflation. If the contract includes a buy-in provision, you should time your contract to cover the period leading to partnership. If you will be eligible to buy-into the practice in two years, then negotiate a two-year contract.

Probationary Period: Note that a portion of the first year may be considered a probationary period, usually two to six months. Not every contract includes a probationary period, but you should negotiate one in your contract. During the probationary period, either party may terminate the agreement for any reason. You may obtain employment in a practice or organization that is not a good fit; you want to be able to terminate the contract without serious ramifications. You should negotiate a clause that excludes any restrictive covenants, such as non-compete clauses, during the probationary period.

Job Description/Duties and Responsibilities: The scope of your job duties should be clearly stated in the contract or as an attachment to the contract. Be certain that any duties that you might be expected to perform, as well as excluded duties, are listed in the contract. If, for example, an OB/GYN's clinic decides to offer abortion services and the physician candidate does not wish to provide this service, the contract will indicate whether or not this is a required duty. By anticipating this as a worst case scenario, a physician can be certain that she is not required to engage in a particular service based on the contract.

This section of the contract may include hours on call, administrative duties, teaching responsibilities, committee work, input in hiring and firing decisions, and explanation of managed care contracts for which you're responsible. It may also outline productivity expectations such as number of patient visits or total billings in a given period of time. Your contract should be very clear about what will be expected of you. You don't want to start a job and learn in the middle of holiday plans that you're expected to be on-call during the holidays. (If you're considering a contract with a hospital or medical institution, be certain to read the policies and procedures, the employee handbook, and the by-laws as these will be attached to your contract.)

Pay attention to call coverage, which should be outlined with specifics. Your contract should indicate a minimum and maximum number of call hours. You should negotiate more pay for extra call coverage. If you enter a field with heavy call duties, you may want your contract to indicate a contingency for increased call coverage. If, for example, a partner becomes ill or disabled and your call coverage is expanded, will you be expected to maintain the expanded coverage? Will you be compensated accordingly? Will the practice hire more physicians to provide relief? This provision may not be important to a pathologist, but an OB/GYN, pediatrician or other specialist with heavy call duty will need to consider this clause carefully.

> **Compensation:** Although you'll be very concerned about this figure, this should not be the only detail you should address. You have many other factors to consider regarding your contract terms. When you are ready to discuss compensation, keep in mind that the compensation should be in line with the market. Do your research. Use the average rate of pay for starting physicians in your specialty and geographic area. (You can purchase physician compensation surveys that indicate these average figures. Compensation surveys cost a few hundred dollars but amount to money well spent. A survey

gives you a more objective idea of what you're worth. The Medical Group Management Association publishes a good survey. Visit www.mgma.com for details.) You can also check trade journals for special issues that publish compensation surveys or advertise for them.

There are several types of compensation models:

Straight productivity: Compensation comes wholly from performance on productivity measures. Productivity measures may include:

Number of patients treated

Number of procedures

Adjusted charges

Total billings

Revenue less overhead

Patient satisfaction ratings

Straight guaranteed compensation: Fixed salary, this is common with physicians employed by institutions.

Equal shares: In this arrangement, revenues left at the end of the fiscal year are divided among shareholders and paid as compensation.

There are also hybrids of compensation that mix productivity or bonus pay with guaranteed compensation.

Be certain you understand the proposed compensation structure, bonus criteria and productivity measures. Ask questions to clarify compensation provisions. If compensation is based on collections, ask questions about the group's collection procedures. Find out what portion of collections is written off. What's the average length on outstanding patient accounts? If you sign with a guaranteed salary, be sure to ask how your compensation structure will change as you gain experience. Your salary increases should be based, at a minimum on the Consumer Price Index, typically four to eight percent, and you should ask that they be based on a higher rate, such as 10-12%. Bonuses can be paid on performance toward goals or percent of salary or collections. If you are negotiating with a tax-exempt employer, bonuses and retirement benefits will be more limited because of IRS and legal restrictions.

When considering compensation, don't overlook the value of group insurance benefits and retirement plans. A position with a lower salary and terrific benefits may be a more lucrative offer than a position with a higher salary and adequate benefits. If the employer offers group benefits that you can opt to purchase, such as disability insurance or life insurance, remember that these benefits are usually much more expensive and difficult to obtain if you're purchasing them as an individual. Plus, purchasing some of these policies with your pre-tax dollars reduces your annual federal income tax. If your employer offers term life insurance, check that the policy is convertible to a permanent policy. This can be an enormous benefit to you as you age.

> **Disability Insurance:** If you're considering joining a practice, inquire about the employer's disability insurance coverage. Remember that when considering disability insurance, an "own-occupation" policy is the most valuable and useful disability policy designation. Also bear in mind that you'll probably want to supplement the group plan with additional individual coverage. If the employer doesn't offer this type of coverage, this benefit may be of minimal value.

> **Sick Leave/Vacation:** Clarify these benefits. How much do you get? When can you access your vacation time? Can you take it all at once? Can you roll your vacation time over to the next year, or will you lose it if you don't take it? Determine

how much flexibility you have with this provision. Female physicians should also inquire about maternity leave, which is usually unpaid.

Malpractice Insurance: Be prepared to get details about the employer's malpractice insurance. Remember that you need to assure yourself that the employer's carrier is obligated to cover you in good faith. You'll need to supplement malpractice insurance polices that can't sustain a $1 million judgment.

Tail coverage: Malpractice tail coverage protects you from claims that are made once you are no longer covered by an employer's malpractice plan after termination. Tail coverage not only protects you, it protects the practice or organization for claims that may arise after your termination. Your employer will insist on tail coverage upon your termination. Tail coverage is extremely expensive – sometimes as much as 150% the cost of your annual malpractice premium – and locating $100,000 to pay for tail coverage upon termination may be a difficult undertaking. Be certain that your contract states who will provide tail coverage. Your employer may balk at paying for tail coverage, but you may be able to negotiate a compromise.

Partnership/Buy-In: Your contract should clearly indicate offers to achieve partnership in the future, if that is an option. The average road to partnership varies by specialty, but verbal promises won't hold up. The specific formula for calculating buy-in cost and a timeline for reaching partnership should be noted in the contract. We advise our clients to aim for a low buy-in and the ability to pay with pre-tax dollars.

When considering a partnership provision, you should ask to see a copy of the stockholder's agreement and financial statements for the practice. Have a Certified Public Accountant (CPA) who specializes in healthcare business review these documents. If the practice is established under multiple entities, know what the partnership offer includes. If the building and the equipment are owned by separate entities inside the practice, do the partnership and the scope of the offer extend to shares of these entities as well, or do they solely cover the accounts receivable? It may seem awkward to discuss these terms now, but you need to be clear on exactly what the offer includes.

Ownership of Records, Accounts Receivable: Your employer will probably try to limit your access to medical records upon termination. If you decide to leave the employer, you may want to notify your patients. You may also want to consider liability issues and continuity of care for patients you'd be leaving behind. Access to your patient's records may provide both. Does your contract allow you this privilege? Who owns the medical records, and how much will you be charged to buy them from the employer after your termination? With this information in your contract from the beginning, you'll always be clear about your rights to own your patients' records. Account receivable ownership is also an issue that should be explicitly stated in your contract.

Assignment: Find out what happens in case of merger or acquisition. Your contract should indicate whether or not it's assignable. Consider this clause carefully. If your employer is bought-out or merges, you may not wish to work for the new employer. The assignment clause may allow the contract to be automatically assigned to the new hospital without your approval in the event of a merger. To prevent this scenario, you can negotiate a clause that allows your contract to expire under certain circumstances, for example upon a merger.

Termination: Termination can be "with cause" or "without cause". Attempt to negotiate a clause that lifts the restrictive covenants and explains what happens to your tail coverage if you terminate without cause. Some of our clients negotiate employer provided tail coverage as a provision that allows the coverage to be paid directly from their salaries in the case of termination without cause or non-renewal of contract.

Under a "with-cause" provision, be certain that the "cause" is defined in writing. Watch for vague language such as "acts deemed harmful to the practice", which may include minor infractions such as dress code violations or tardiness. This clause is extremely important as a termination "with cause" follows you around for your entire career. It must be disclosed when you apply for malpractice insurance and will affect your premiums. Request a clause in the contract that allows a due process hearing for termination with cause. A requirement of a majority vote by the partners is another important safeguard to request. Many of our clients also negotiate for a 60 day notice of termination. This important feature allows terminated physicians the opportunity to locate additional employment in the interim. If a provision for immediate cause is included, be certain that the causes are clearly stated (For example: "committing a crime").

You'll also want written explanation of what happens to unpaid salary, medical records (Can you access them? Can you contact patients?), and incentive compensation in the event of termination. Request that compensation be paid through your effective termination date. You will want to include language that allows for other employment after termination.

As previously mentioned, your termination clause should also define who will pay for "tail" coverage upon your termination.

Buy-Out Provision: A buy-out provision protects you in certain circumstances such as bankruptcy or dissolution of the group. A buy-out provision can also help if the practice loses its largest contract. This clause should state the specific buy-out formula and the conditions under which you can initiate a buy-out.

Restrictive Covenants (Non-compete Clauses): Clearly this clause, which limits where and when you can practice, is not in your best interest. Try to ask that it be deleted or, at a minimum, limit the restrictions so that they're more favorable to you. A non-compete clause that limits you for a few years and under a five mile radius from the primary office may be a reasonable restriction depending on your specialty. If a large practice has multiple offices, the restrictive covenant could exclude you from practicing in the entire city if the restriction is not limited to one location.

Moonlighting: Physicians can supplement their incomes nicely with moonlighting opportunities, such as speaking engagements and publishing books. This might be a critical feature of your contract if you plan to do business activities outside of the group. Even if you don't think you plan to moonlight, you should be careful of this clause. A contract with language that prohibits moonlighting may even prevent you from receiving income for speaking or publishing articles. If you decide to publish a book and your contract prohibits moonlighting, technically you could be terminated, and the money earned would belong to the group. Although the practice is probably not trying to limit you from this type of work, the moonlighting clause should be clear about your options for earning additional income. You should negotiate a clause that allows you to practice outside the legitimate business interests of the group. This will protect the group's financial interest while allowing you to earn significant additional income.

Other Benefits: Your contract may include other benefits to consider when evaluating an offer, such as travel expenses, professional membership fees, seminar fees, hospital privileges, beeper, cell phone, association dues, publication allowances, and other reasonable business expenses. Many physicians also negotiate employer-covered CME expenses, including travel and meals while in attendance.

Confidentiality: Keep the details of your contract confidential. Disclosing the terms of your contract could lead to termination.

When considering a contract, remember that salary and incentive are only two factors. Consider other benefits including moving allowances, sign-on bonuses, assistance paying-off student loans, housing allowance, flexible work hours, and flexible vacation. Weigh the overall offer, not merely the salary and incentives.

Make a list of any questions you have regarding terms in the contract. Be sure you are clear on everything and get everything in writing. If you don't understand something in the contract, get an explanation from the employer. Whether you understand the terms or not, they're part of a legal document that will bind you and your employer.

Dr. Benovsky Seals the Deal

Dr. Benovsky considered Women's Health Associates her top choice. She had a dinner appointment to meet with the managing partner, Dr. Alleman, to discuss their proposed contract. Dr. Benovsky was thrilled that her first choice was considering her. She arrived at the restaurant a few minutes before the dinner appointment, nervous but enthusiastic. She was ready to get a contract and start making money. Dr. Alleman greeted Dr. Benovsky and chatted with her over an appetizer. Dr. Alleman was very complimentary of her work and informed Dr. Benovsky that the partnership typically offered physicians of her caliber a starting salary of $140,000. "That sounds good," remarked Dr. Benovsky, and the two physicians spoke about the practice and the other contract details over dinner.

The next day, a colleague told Dr. Benovsky that she had purchased a salary survey for physicians in her specialty and geographic regions. After reviewing the survey, the colleague realized that she would have to lower her expectations if she continued to pursue work in her preferred city. Dr. Benovsky consulted the survey and was crestfallen to find that she had verbally agreed to $25,000 below the average for OB/GYN's in the city where Women's Health Associates practiced. She knew verbal contracts weren't enforceable, so she attempted to change the salary clause in her contract. She soon received an angry email response from Dr. Alleman rescinding her offer.

Follow the Negotiation Timeline

1. Hire a contract review advisor.

2. Receive draft of contract.

3. Review the proposed contract with your advisor.

4. Respond to the proposed contract draft.

5. Meet with the employer in person

6. Negotiate the terms.

7. Continue the review process.

8. Finalize the contract.

1. Hire a Contract Review Advisor

You need a team of advisors to assist you in this endeavor. Engage the services of a professional contract reviewer who specializes in employment contracts. As we said earlier, medicine is business. And a solid contract is the basis for good business.

2. Receive Draft of Contract

Once you have identified employment opportunities that you would like to consider, the employer will present you with a contract draft. Do not comment immediately on the proposed contract. Making comment on the contract may limit your negotiating power. If you meet with the managing partner or an employer's representative to discuss an offer, do not agree to any terms. Even though verbal agreements aren't enforceable, your comments may create an understanding of acceptance by the employer. After you meet with the employer, write an e-mail to the contact person and recap the discussion. List the aspects of the proposed contract that you particularly liked and those that you did not like. This will create a written record of your meeting that the employer can review with his attorney when drafting the contract. Ask your advisors to review the response before you send it to the employer.

3. Review the Proposed Contract with a Professional

Even though money may still be tight, you should never skip this step. Your contract will dictate every term of your employment, and a poorly negotiated contract could be a detriment to your career and could severely limit your opportunities as a physician. You should meet with your advisor before the first contract meeting with the employer and afterward. An advisor will be able to help you negotiate the best deal from behind the scenes as well as interpret the contract for you. With your advisor's assistance, you'll also create a strategy for the contract negotiation. Your advisor will help you determine how to respond to your contract draft.

4. Respond to the Contract

Most of our clients start off with a contract that is more of a wish-list than anything else. Entering negotiations with a wish-list is unrealistic and may cause you to lose out on the provisions that are most important to you. If a parking spot is something that you can't live without, then request it. On the other hand, if the ability to limit your call coverage is more important, be certain that you know these priorities before entering negotiations. We often suggest that our clients choose the four or five most important issues in the contract and attempt to negotiate for those items.

5. Meet with the Employer in Person

After meeting with your advisor, schedule a meeting with the employer to present your proposed changes. Many of our clients also respond to the proposed contract via e-mail. We always recommend that any email responses be reviewed by one of your professional advisors before you send them.

6. Negotiate Terms with the Other Party

If you're negotiating with an employer-physician, you'll typically negotiate with the decision maker. In a hospital or other large institution, you may be negotiating with a representative who is not empowered to make decisions. Large organizations are typically less likely to vary terms, but this doesn't mean that the terms are non-negotiable. If employers prefer that their contracts be similarly crafted, you usually can submit changes and attach them to the contracts as long as they are clearly labeled, identified, signed and noted as attachments in the contract. If you find that the employer is unwilling to negotiate, you may decide to consider opportunities elsewhere.

The negotiation process is your opportunity to determine if you share goals with the prospective employer. If the terms that are important to you aren't included in the contract, and the employer won't add them, then your goals may not mesh with the employer's, and you may need to seek opportunity elsewhere.

Contract negotiation should be a win-win; you want to get the best for yourself while being fair to the practice or employer. With your advisor's assistance, you'll know what your non-negotiables are and what's open for discussion. Approach the negotiation in a respectful and professional manner, but ask for what you want. If it's really important, go ahead and make the request.

Make a file for all paperwork related to the negotiation and the contract. Put all correspondences including drafts of contracts and handwritten notes in one file. Date everything. If you're working with an advisor, you'll have someone on your side along the way helping you make the most of the negotiation.

7. Continue the Review Process

The review process may take a few rounds. Your advisor will guide you through the reviews. Remember during this process that the items you identified as non-negotiable are just that. If the process drags on, do not give up your priorities. If you can't get a contract that is fair to you and the employer, you may need to seek other opportunities.

8. Finalize

Once you've reached an agreement, finalize your contract. All parties should sign and date the final draft. Give one copy to your advisor for safekeeping and file your copy. Although most relationships are trouble–free, you should be able to access your contract at any time should a dispute arise. A well-negotiated contact will make the transition from residency to practice a pleasant and lucrative one.

Completing your medical training is a major accomplishment that will reap big rewards. Negotiating a fair and lucrative contract is also a major accomplishment that, when undertaken with professional assistance and patience, will yield equally big dividends.

Misstep

If you ask for a provision, be wary if the response is, "That has never happened here, you don't need that." If you have a concern that has never been an issue with the employer, then there is no reason for them not to accommodate your request.

Please note that this chapter addresses general concepts relating to contract negotiation and does not offer legal advice. The laws that govern contracts vary from state to state. You should consult an attorney before executing any negotiation strategies to insure that you accomplish your goals.

Final Thoughts

Medicine is not a do-it-yourself venture. It would be quite alarming if a heart patient showed up at a medical school library, checked out a textbook on bypass surgery, and went home to try to repair his coronary arteries. Even if he spent months reading medical journals and heart surgeon websites, watched surgeries on the Discovery Channel, and listened to surgeon talk radio, the prospect of do-it-yourself medicine is too absurd to fathom.

As residents you know that a good physician's service lies not only in the information, but in the experience and expertise. The same goes for financial planning in accumulating and preserving your wealth. The purpose of this book is not to encourage you to take up tax planning, wealth protection, and asset protection as do-it-yourself prospects. Instead, we hope to help you be a more effective partner with your financial team.

As you move through your residency and move closer toward realizing your dreams, you also move closer to meeting your earning potential. Making sound financial decisions and solid financial plans will help you achieve your financial goals even sooner. We've attempted to provide you with a base for your financial planning.

We realize that this book may have raised more questions for you than it answered. That's because financial planning, like medicine, is not a one size fits all proposition. When making any decisions about your finances, we strongly urge you to perform your due diligence and engage a professional. A financial advisor will be a valuable addition to your team of advisors throughout your career, as your needs change and as your career progresses. Good advisors share characteristics of good physicians: strong interpersonal skills, the ability to assess not only your primary financial concern but your overall financial health, and the ability to recommend the best course of action. A financial advisor who specializes in physicians' needs is your greatest ally in initiating and maintaining a financial plan, helping you to create a road map, and staying on track to the financial rewards you've worked hard to realize.

We wish you a successful and rewarding career and hope that we've helped you enhance your Financial Fund of Knowledge.

Printed in the United States
216755BV00001B/2/A

9 780979 279409